The Lion and the Eagle

Europe 1937

The Lion and the Eagle

Reminiscences
of
Polish Second World War
Veterans
in
Scotland

Dr Diana M Henderson LLB TD FSA Scot
Editor

Cualann Press

ISBN 0 9535036 4 X

First Edition October 2001

British Library Cataloguing in Publication Data. A catalogue record of this book is available at the British Library.

Printed by Bell & Bain, Glasgow

Published by:
Cualann Press, 6 Corpach Drive, Dunfermline, KY12 7XG, Scotland
Email: cualann@btinternet.com
Website: http://users.ouvip.com/cualann

Contents

Illustrations

Historical Scene

I would like to set the historical scene – the backdrop for the stories these remarkable Polish Veterans have to tell us.

On 1st September 1939, Germany invaded Poland. Seventeen days later, Soviet troops crossed the Polish border from the east 'to protect their fellow Slavs'. After a heroic fight on two fronts, the Polish Government crossed the border into Romania, and there its members were interned.

During these dramatic events, as we shall read, a number of Poles escaped across the Romanian, Czech and Hungarian borders and eventually joined the Polish Forces in France.

Other Poles were captured by the advancing Soviet Army and taken as forced labour to Siberia and Northern Russia. The Polish Nation was divided: this effectively created the strands of two stories.

Poles in France formed and trained. Some were sent to the defence of Norway and were at Narvik with the British in the spring of 1940. In May 1940, when Germany attacked France, Free Polish Forces prepared to defend Paris. With the fall of France, some of the Polish troops crossed into Switzerland where they were interned. Others escaped from French ports to Britain. Many were sent to Scotland and there was good reason for this.

Lost in the Battle for France in 1940 was the whole of the cream of the Highland Territorial Army, the 51st Highland Division, which had been forced to surrender at St

Valery-en-Caux. This Division was reconstituted overnight by simply renaming the 9th Scottish Division, then stationed at home, as the 51st Highland Division. In Scotland, now completely unprotected against invasion and the real threat of German attacks, the newly arrived Poles were warmly welcomed. They immediately set to work defending Scotland.

There was, however, no military infrastructure to accommodate them and they were left in our inhospitable climate, largely to their own devices, to live in tents, build their own camps, patrol the coastline and build coastal defences.

Filling sandbags for Coastal Defences (© Fife Council Museums East)

These Polish Service men and women made a lasting impression in Scotland during those early years. They could be seen in Cupar, Leven, Milnathort, Auchtermuchty, Crawford, Biggar, Douglas, Duns, Kelso, Forres, Perth, Tayport, Lossiemouth, Arbroath, Forfar, and Carnoustie. There were Polish Schools of Engineering, a Polish Staff College, a Polish Record Office and a Polish Parachute Training School.

Many Scots, especially ladies, were astounded by Polish good looks and by Polish courtesy. When the Poles left for D Day and the campaign in North West Europe in 1944, a large number of Scottish girls were heartbroken.

Meanwhile, the Polish Forces in the Soviet Union had not fared so well. When Germany invaded Russia in 1941, the Soviets and the Poles became allies overnight. Poles were released from forced labour and a Polish Army was raised in Southern Russia. The Soviet Government, however, was reluctant to arm and equip Polish Forces on Russian soil and in 1942, in a situation of deteriorating Polish-Soviet relations, the Polish Army in the Soviet Union was evacuated to the Middle East and placed under British command. This Army fought with distinction in North Africa and Italy.

The final breakdown of Polish-Soviet relations was in April 1943, when the Germans announced the discovery of a mass grave in the Forest of Katyn, near Smolensk, containing the bodies of 4,000 Polish Officers murdered by the Soviets.

In the west, Polish Forces served with distinction on the sea, on the land and in the air. A number of Polish Squadrons was formed as part of the Royal Air Force and they had an outstanding success rate. Polish Infantry and

Armoured Forces landed in France shortly after D-day in 1944 and Polish Airborne Forces landed at Arnhem.

In 1945, the Polish Army, which had formerly been based in the Soviet Union, and the Polish Forces which had trained and served in Scotland, were joined in the United Kingdom. However, the January 1945 Yalta Agreement meant that many of these men and women could not return to their homes because of boundary changes and the establishment of a Stalinist sphere of influence over Poland.

A large number of Poles chose to stay in the United Kingdom and, happily, a large number of those chose to stay in Scotland. In the following pages are some of their stories of survival against the odds. It is a privilege to record them.

Dr Diana M Henderson, Honorary Research Director
The Scots at War Trust 2001

Preface

Embassy of The Republic of Poland
47 Portland Place
London

The United Kingdom has a special place in the hearts of the Poles. Firstly, because of their common history and secondly, because of the events of World War II, including the tragic occupation of Poland by two totalitarian powers in 1939 and the fall of France in 1940. All of this meant that Polish dreams of a free, democratic Poland were in tune with the British.

I remember Professor Bronislaw Geremek, former Minister of Foreign Affairs, telling me about his being outside the British Embassy in Warsaw on 3rd September 1939 where Poles demonstrated their joy when Britain declared war on Germany. The only power then able to stand against Nazi Germany was Britain.

For many Poles, the UK became their second homeland and London was the seat of the wartime Polish Government in exile. During times of war, Britain was Poland's closest ally. The Polish and the British soldiers fought together for the freedom of their countries and the freedom of Europe and the men whose stories are recorded in this book are Poland's heroes. For many Poles after the war, 'the London government' meant the Government of the free, democratic Poland. There are lots of Polish graves in the British cemeteries, and almost every large town in this country had, or still has, a Polish Club.

Today's relations between Poland and the United Kingdom are excellent. Indeed, the second half of this millennium year has seen just a few initiatives in Polish-British relations that can support this statement. These were, for example, the handing over of an Enigma encoding machine to the Polish Prime Minister by HRH The Duke of York 'as a symbol of British thanks' for the role of Polish mathematicians who made an outstanding contribution towards breaking the enigma's code by British analysts at Bletchley Park in 1939; the unveiling in London, in September, of a statue of General Wladyslaw Sikorski, the war time Prime Minister of the Polish Government in exile and the Supreme Commander of the Polish Armed Forces; and, the setting up of a joint Polish-British commission of historians to examine British archives in order to provide evidence of the contribution of Polish Intelligence to the Allied war effort during World War II. These initiatives prove that, after all this time, Polish efforts have been appreciated and that the truth about the difficult past will be known to the public.

Representatives of Polish Veterans present their memories in this book. There are common factors in their stories; they found their shelter on friendly British soil; they served in many areas when they arrived in Britain and they enjoyed the kindness of the Scottish people.

If Europe had not been divided by Yalta, Poland, and other central European states which found themselves, against their will, on the wrong side of 'the iron curtain', would most probably have participated in the Euro-Atlantic structures. Nevertheless, Poles were never comfortable with the imposed system and, as a result, Poland was in the forefront of the transformations in Central and Eastern Europe. These transformations have been achieved in a way in which Timothy Garton Ash calls a 'revolution', a peaceful revolution through reforms.

Poland's membership of the North Atlantic Alliance may be described as crossing the political Rubicon in the process of anchoring Poland among the group of countries collectively referred to as 'the west'. But it will be the membership of the European Union that will finally secure a comprehensive and favourable environment for Poland to achieve further economic development, her widely understood security and her sense of being part of a community of states with which we share a cultural and historic heritage, as well as common values.

I would like to thank everybody involved in The Scots at War Trust for their efforts to collect and record this important historical material concerning Polish Armed Forces in Scotland during World War II. Especially, I would like to express my deepest thanks to Dr Diana Henderson, for her personal involvement in the project.

Dr Stanisław Komorowski
Ambassador of the Republic of Poland

Key Dates: Polish Forces in Scotland

1939

1st September: Germany invades Poland

9th September: Franco-Polish Military Agreement allowing Polish troops to form and train on French soil

17th September: Soviet troops cross the Polish border

18th September: The Polish Government crosses the border into Romania

18th November: Anglo-Polish Agreement organising Polish Naval units alongside the Royal Navy

1940

11th April: Anglo-Polish Agreement regarding the formation of Polish Air Force units in UK

April – June: A combined British, French and Polish Force sees action against the Germans at Narvik in Norway and is eventually evacuated

10th May: Germany attacks France

26th May – 3rd June: Evacuation of Allied troops from France at Dunkirk

12th June: 51st Highland Division surrenders at St Valery; 2nd Polish Rifle Division crosses the border into Switzerland and is interned; the first Polish troops reach Scotland

5th August: Anglo-Polish Military Agreement regulating the conditions of Polish Military Service in the UK

1941

24th February: Signing of agreement to form the Polish Medical School at the University of Edinburgh

22nd June: Germany attacks Soviet Russia.

30th July: Polish-Soviet agreement on full military cooperation. All Polish citizens to be released by the Soviets and a Polish Army to be formed in the USSR

1942
Decision to evacuate the Polish Army from the USSR and to take this Polish Army under British command in the Middle East

1943
April: Germans discover the bodies of over 4000 Polish Officers murdered by the Soviets in a mass grave in the Forest at Katyn near Smolensk. Diplomatic relations between USSR and Poland broken off
4th July: The Prime Minister of Poland, General Sikorski, killed in an air crash at Gibraltar

1944
June: Polish Forces take part in the Allied landings in France
September: Polish Airborne Forces land at Arnhem in Holland; Polish Forces in action in Italy

1945
8th May: Victory in Europe

1946
Polish Resettlement Corps formed in UK

The Scots at War Trust Seminar

Sir Winston Churchill and General S Sikorski inspecting a marchpast in pouring rain (© Fife Council Museums East)

Part I

Recent Accounts

Captain Tadeusz Apfel-Czaszka
1st Polish Armoured Division

Edinburgh

My family lived in Lwów which is now in the Ukraine where, during the First World War, my father was a medical student. He became a Lieutenant in the Austrian Army and served in a Hungarian unit. However, he refused to swear allegiance to Emperor Franz Joseph of Austria and he was greatly distrusted as a result. He became a drama producer between the wars and during the Second World War, after first escaping to Hungary, he was made a prisoner of war in Germany.

In 1939, I was just finishing High School and I was on a fishing holiday in the west of Poland when the war started. I volunteered to enlist in my father's unit and I came back to Lwów where I joined my father, who could speak Hungarian, and together we went to Hungary on army transport.

The Hungarians were very good to us but on Christmas Eve 1939, I left the camp that we were in and I made my way to France to join the Polish Army which was forming there. We went to Brittany to a terrible old First World War camp to form up and train. Here I joined the 1st

Grenadier Division from part of which the Polish Highland Brigade was formed.

We were training to fight the Germans in Finland. On the 27th of April 1940, however, we left Brest in a French transport and we were sent to Norway to fight the Germans. From Brest the convoy assembled at Greenock on the Clyde and we then sailed north and arrived first at Tromső. We transferred to British destroyers and we went ashore further down the coast. Our Battalion was in reserve and our job was to catch spies, to guard the German deserters and to guard ammunition. When the force was evacuated from Norway in June 1940, we once more boarded the destroyers, transferred to a luxury liner returning from taking evacuee children to Canada, and returned to Brest. When we arrived there, France was in collapse, the German guns were only seventeen miles away and we were told that arrangements would be made to hand us over to the Germans as prisoners of war. We were not prepared for this to be done and in order to make our escape, we set out on a boat going to Bordeaux in Free France. On the way, the boat was captured by the British and we were sent to Southampton and on to Liverpool. We were then sent North by train into Scotland and I spent my first night sleeping in the school at Coatbridge. At Coatbridge, the people were very welcoming and they did everything that they could to help us. From there we went on to Bellahouston Park where we lived in tents, and later to Douglas West.

I remember that the weather was good and I felt that I already knew a lot about Scotland. In High School we had a good education and we were taught all about Bonnie Prince

Charlie and the many Scots throughout history who had served the Kings of Poland.

On the 1st of September 1940, the 1st Polish Infantry Brigade, comprising the Independent Highland Battalion, the 2nd Battalion and the 3rd Battalion, moved to Biggar. I remember that the mud was terrible. The 2nd Battalion went to Tentsmuir Forest near St Andrews and the 3rd Battalion went to Cupar. I went to Tentsmuir where I lived in the school at Tayport. Here our job was to guard against the expected German invasion which we firmly believed would come. We built blockhouses and concrete obstacles, defended the coast with our French machine guns and trained.

In 1942, General Maczeck formed the 1st Polish Armoured Division. I joined this Division and transferred to Kelso and Duns. The Dragoons were in Galashiels. Here in the Borders of Scotland, I began to learn tank driving, radio operating and shooting and we were issued with Sherman Tanks. We then moved to Newmarket and we were joined by Czechs and Free French forces. For a time we returned to the Scottish Borders and I remember visits from Montgomery and Eisenhower. Finally, we moved to Bridlington where, before we left, we were given our pay in invasion francs.

From there, it was on to Aldershot and Tilbury docks where we boarded Liberty boats and we landed on the invasion beaches in Normandy in France on the 28th July 1944. The beaches were all marked to indicate where we were to go. In Normandy, our first town was Bayeux. At this time we were bombed by US Flying Fortresses who mistook us for the enemy and we lost a number of men and tanks.

Building Coastal Defences in Scotland (© Fife Council Museums East)

I remember that it was a beautiful hot summer. We attacked through forests in bitter fighting against German Tiger and Panther tanks and eight out of our sixteen tanks were destroyed. One of the problems with the Sherman tanks was that they went on fire very easily. I lost my best friend when his tank was hit by an 88mm German gun.

We then took part in the big battle at Falaise and at this point we were attached to the 1st Canadian Army. The Germans were surrounded on three sides like a bottle and the Polish Division was chosen for the job of being the cork in the bottle to cut the Germans off completely. In the confusion, we had no time to get more petrol or ammunition, we got lost in the darkness and we found ourselves behind the German lines. With us at this time were 3000 German prisoners. The enemy began shelling us with rockets and the Allies tried to re-supply us from the air. At one point, a German Captain came forward and a two-hour truce was organised to clear the wounded. For three days we fought on with no more petrol or ammunition and we were eventually told to throw away any souvenirs that we had and to prepare to surrender. However, at last the Canadians broke through and large numbers of Germans were captured in the pocket. The destruction was terrible. It was very hot and there was the most awful smell coming from the thousands of bodies of dead German transport horses which covered the battlefield. I remember that and the pitiful calls of the cattle in the fields needing to be milked.

There was a lot of hard fighting and I was wounded when my tank was destroyed. By this stage there were four men and not five to each tank because of the shortage of numbers. After Falaise, we had two days' rest and then we moved on very quickly north through France. We went on into Belgium where again my tank was lost during the fighting at Ypres when a German 88mm shell ricocheted off the road and opened up the front of the vehicle. I remember seeing the rounding up of those local women who had fraternized with the Germans. The people shaved their heads and painted them red. We were told not to interfere.

Because the Germans had blown up the tunnels at Antwerp, we swung east and then north into Holland where we liberated Breda. We did not use mortars so as not to damage the city and I can remember we were warmly welcomed with flags and bunting by the people and the Burgomaster.

We then settled down to face the enemy on the other side of the River Maas. The infantry were in front and we lived in houses further back. I stayed with a Dutch family. The husband was a tailor. In the house there was still a German uniform and a German helmet which the Germans had left in their haste to get out. The food was very bad. The bread was so hard you could break the window with it. But the Dutch were very kind and there were many marriages between the Polish soldiers and Dutch girls.

That winter I was made a Corporal and I was sent to Officer school at Catterick after which I finished as a Cadet Officer in Crieff. In 1945, I was sent to the Polish Staff College at Cupar as a supply officer and I then moved on to the Polish Record Office at Kinghorn. As the war ended, some of my friends joined the British Army but I had had enough of army life.

I put down my name to go back to Poland, but I got a letter from my father through a contact in Sweden telling me not to return. Every letter that we sent to Poland was opened and some of those who received letters from the United Kingdom lost their jobs. In Scotland, it was difficult for Polish servicemen to get a job as the miners in Fife were very much against us with their 'Poles go home' campaign, so I started as a labourer and then went to work on the buses for twenty years. For fifteen years I drove a Number 41 bus in Edinburgh. I married a Scottish girl and we now often go back to Poland where we have many friends.

Captain Tadeusz Apfel-Czaszka (second from right) with fellow veterans and Archbishop Keith O'Brien (left) at the Polish Church, Edinburgh

Zbigniew Budzyński
5th Polish Infantry Division

Haddington

I was born in 1920 in Lublin in Poland. When I finished Highers at school I was obliged to work for two or three weeks in a work camp organised and led by the Army. On 16th August 1939, I reported to the camp on the northern border of Poland and East Prussia. I worked with other school leavers from all over Poland on a fortification near Osowill, an old Russian fortress.

On Friday 1st September 1939, while at work, we heard coming from the North the roar of many engines. Shortly afterwards we could see, low over the horizon, many black points which were soon transformed into low flying German Dornier bombers. Heavily loaded, they swayed gently as they flew, slowly gaining height. We could see the pilots' faces; we could have shot them down with catapults even, if we had had catapults. They disappeared flying south.

Some days later, we were evacuated east to Lida where there was a big depot of an Infantry Division. By then the Germans occupied a number of regions in Poland. Lads from those regions could not return home, so at Lida we were all mobilised and conscripted into the Army. A

Divisional School was organised for Infantry Reserve Officers and we became the last cadets of this school.

On 17th September 1939, the Red Army invaded Poland. In the early evening of that Sunday we marched out of barracks to the railway station and to war. The train moved; we were going – where? At one stop, one of our sections was detailed to keep order in a nearby village where local youths and communists had begun attacking Poles. We kept order, but the Soviet tanks were almost on the village square when we escaped on a lorry.

In the early evening we arrived at Grodno where, tired and hungry, we went to sleep. Soon, we were awakened by the crunch of tank tracks, and, rifles in hand, we joined a group of soldiers and made Molotov Cocktails. We grabbed a bottle or two and went hunting. Four tanks were destroyed. We rejoined our unit and took up positions on the bank of the river and the night passed quietly. Then we had to run. The Soviets were firing across the river with artillery and machine gun fire and they had infantry with boats. We marched, avoiding Soviet tanks, until we reached the Lithuanian border.

We crossed the border on the night of the 23rd September 1939 and for the next nine or ten months we were interned by the Lithuanians. In about May 1940, a referendum was held to decide if Lithuania, with other Baltic states, should join the Soviet Union as Republics of the Soviet Union. The Soviet Union had had military bases in Lithuania since October and November 1939 so that voting was well prepared; the official count was over 91% in favour.

Until that point, we had been guarded by Lithuanian soldiers with a Soviet NKVD[1] standing beside them. Shortly afterwards, there was no Lithuanian guard and we were truly in Soviet hands. Deportation to Russia came soon after. We marched with our belongings to the station and were loaded into cattle trucks which were shut and bolted. Two or three days later, we were unloaded in the middle of nowhere and we then marched five or six miles to a camp which was called Pawliszczew Bor near the small township of Juchnowo in the Smolensk region.

We spent about ten months in that camp. There was no work apart from normal camp duties. To start with, we had to attend 'Political Hours' which included propaganda films telling us how good life was in the Soviet Union. The only intelligent and educated officer in the camp was the Major Camp Commandant who led the political hours; the rest of the camp staff had little more than three or four years of primary school education and we had great fun arguing with them. They had no opinions of their own and their replies were always a recitation of one or other of the well-known communists. We were well treated although the food was very poor. We were told, 'You'll live, but you will never think of making love.' Every four weeks or so, we had a steam bath in a washhouse that we built for ourselves.

Propaganda and political hours died away after Christmas 1940 and the whisper of being exchanged with the Germans for people from Soviet occupied territories died with it. What next? Soon it came. In the spring, May

---

[1] Narodnyi Kommissariat Vnutrennickh Del (People's Commissariat for Internal Affairs)

perhaps, of 1941, after showers, delousing and searches we marched. We were put on a train and this time we went north. Soon we passed Leningrad and when we passed Kandalakka we knew that we were heading for Murmansk and beyond. For two or three days we journeyed on, stop, go, stop, go, until we came to the area of Murmansk where we marched into another camp. Nothing was said to us as to where we were going or what was to happen to us.

Unloading took place surrounded by barbed wire, gates and watchtowers. There were camps inside camps. Weeks, I think, were spent here. Then we marched again, this time down the hill to the town and port of Murmansk, gateway to the Russian north with the Arctic Ocean and the seaway to the north coast of Siberia. When we got to the port, we found the rusting hulk of a ship called the *Clara Zetkin,* the name of an eminent German Communist. At the foot of the gangway we learnt our fate from the NKVD officer who had been with us since we arrived in Lithuania. With a smile on his face he told us, 'Where you are going, lads, there is no return from there; you will not see your Poland again.' There was no comment on our side and, quiet and depressed, we boarded the boat.

Once we were all aboard, we sailed eastwards. The White Sea was calm and now and then floating ice scraped or hit the side of the ship. Eventually we arrived and dropped anchor off the coast of Ponoy. An old tug with two box-like barges took us to the landing stage made of planks laid on wooden poles hammered into the bottom of the sea. There was nothing there, just a fishing village with a few buildings where the guards lived. Two large tents with bunks and an iron stove at the end of each one were to be our 'homes'. There were about 2000 of us. We were divided into groups of one hundred men. Two hundred of us were left in camp and told that we would start work as a transporting column while the rest of our mates were marched inland. In the Arctic, in summer, the sun never sets and our days consisted of breakfast of tea and bread, work, a second meal of thin soup and oats, tea in the evening, and sleep.

Every day after breakfast we shouldered bags full of provisions or tools and set out to march six to eight miles. Guards with rifles and dogs marched at the side of the column. Before every march there was the warning, 'A step left or a step right will be taken as an attempt to escape and we will shoot.' It was a march across rough land where there were no roads or paths. At the end of the march, we met the rest of our mates who were employed building an airfield. They lived under the Arctic sky and built small shelters with coats, blankets and a few rocks. By comparison, we were lucky as we had tents with bunks and our food was cooked. We made trips to the airfield every twenty-four hours carrying 200 sacks which were ready every morning, and this went on for a few days. One day I met a friend from school in Lublin, an older man who was a Sergeant in the Artillery and who had fought the Russians in the war in 1920. He said, 'We will never survive winter here,' so four or five of us planned to make an escape, 500 kilometres to Finland. As we had no food, we started collecting and stealing.

One morning there were no sacks ready and we saw two boats standing off with tugs and barges loading people.

Then a long column of Russian prisoners comprising hundreds of men, women, children, cats and dogs came by our camp. It took an hour or more for them to pass. A few hours later, our friends came back and we were put on boats and taken to Archangel. News of war reached us. At the bottom of the gangway stood the same officer who was at Murmansk. One of our lads said to him, 'Well friend, we are going back to Poland.' The Russian looked at him and spat on the ground and said, 'A dog is your friend.'

We were once more put on trains. I remember that there was a beautiful barrel of herring which we started to eat. The problem was that there was about one bucket of water between forty men. It was August and hot. The train stopped in the middle of nowhere and we began marching. Some of the guards were knocked over as 2000 men fought for water.

We marched into a lovely summer manoeuvres' camp of the Soviet Army with loudspeakers playing martial music. On the first night there were guards and we were locked in. On parade, those who were Polish Officers were asked to come forward; there were about fifty or sixty and they stayed with us. The next morning we were told, 'We are fighting the Germans. Polish and Soviets will fight together.' We were also informed that somebody from the Polish Government was coming. We had no guards after that; we were free. The camp was situated in beautiful woods where we could go berry picking. We were given a loaf of bread between two and two dried fish and we marched again to the railway. The truck doors were left open and we went south. We did not know where we were and there was a lot of stopping and starting. Whenever we stopped we tried to scrounge food.

Eventually we arrived at Tatiszezewo near Saratov on the Volga where there was a Polish recruiting camp with tables where we queued up and signed on with the 5th Infantry Division. We were living in tents but in September and October it was beginning to get cold and we went to a wood to cut trees. At the end of October, those with Highers were picked out and became cadets in a School for Reserve Officers of the Infantry. General Sikorski arrived. We had Russian rifles and we spent our first free Christmas in the snow. We could hear the guns in the distance and some Russian cavalry came through our area with bare sabres in their hands and some men with no saddles.

We were given wonderful British uniforms, boots and woollen socks, vests, long johns, jerseys, forage caps and British webbing. We were then moved to the Fergana Valley in the Hindu Kush. I remember that it was muddy and that our education in our Officer school went on until May 1942 when we returned to our companies as Cadet Officers.

In February and March 1942, we heard that the Polish Army was being evacuated and in February the first lot of men left Russia and went to the Middle East. A man on a pushbike arrived, we were marched back to camp and we only had a few hours to get ready. Everything was taken off us, we were given British and New Zealand food, we were put on a train that went to the eastern shores of the Caspian Sea to Krosnowodsk. A boat came and began loading people. Eventually, there were so many people on the boat that you could not move. We sailed for Iran where I remember spending two or three days on the beach and we then went by lorry to Iraq. It was our first Christmas really free and everybody got drunk. We then moved to Kirkuk in the Kurdish region where we were reorganised into a British style formation under British Command. So, I had spent Christmas 1939 in Lithuania, 1940 in the USSR, 1941 with the Polish Army in the USSR, 1942 in Iraq and in 1943 we went to the Lebanon.

We went right through Baghdad and crossed the desert in lorries to Palestine. The Bren Carriers were sent to Basra by train and then were loaded into boats and came by sea to Haifa. I got sick and had to go to hospital while my battalion went to Lebanon for mountain training. I found a friend and was attached to a Machine Gun unit for two weeks. I remember that while I was in the area I visited all of the holy places and I spent that Christmas of 1943 in Lebanon.

On New Year's Day 1944, we went to Egypt and stayed in El Kassassin Barracks and waited for transport to Italy. I got a three-day pass and saw the Pyramids. I then sailed for Italy. Near Crete, the ship was in a collision; rivets flew across the cabins and the ship listed heavily. However, the damage was repaired and eventually we arrived at Taranto. I remember it was raining and muddy. We had nothing with us, not even rifles. We took the train north to Canossa and I was at Campobasso in the spring of 1944.

My battalion went into the line eastwards of Monte Cassino as Battalion Reserve patrolling no man's land, some of which was marked by white tapes. We used to listen to the German radio station, Wanda. They would say, 'Come on

Polish boys, the Russians are coming,' but it was good music and everybody sang Lilie Marlene. We were there for about three weeks and then we went to the rear for a rest. As it was not really work for Bren Carriers and our anti-tank guns were not much use, half of our platoon and half of our anti-tank platoon were sent to Monte Cassino to build a supply store for the battalion. The other two halves were formed as a machine gun platoon. We were given a company of mules with Cypriot drivers. We had to load everything into bags which had to balance on the backs of the mules. We waited until it was dark and then every night we had to go across the valley and through the olive groves with ammunition, food and water. It was a pretty exhausting two-hour trek with the Germans shelling intermittently twenty-four hours a day although quite a number of their shells were dud.

Every unit had its own company of mules; it was all a bit chaotic really. The Germans could hear us very well and the second time we did the journey, we were caught by mortar fire after we crossed the bridge and got on to 'the road of Polish Sappers'. A few mules were killed. The Military Police had a big chain across the path leading through the valley to Monte Cassino and I thought to myself, 'If we go first and we go quickly, we will be OK.' After that it was uneventful.

And then came the night of our attack. All of the infantry companies had been marching past us the day before. H Hour was 11 p.m. and from 10 p.m. everything was dead silent. It was dry, nice warm weather with not a sound. Everybody was tense waiting for the barrage. One gun fired and then there was silence. Then all the guns opened up. It was like daylight and the ground was moving beneath our feet. We waited until 10 a.m. and the first casualties came through. We stood at the side and watched to see who the wounded were. There was dust everywhere. It was a quiet day but in the early evening the lorries came with munitions and water. The Sappers put down a smoke screen and then we went up with supplies. We could hear the mortars firing and the first attack had to be withdrawn because they ran out of munitions and water.

The second attack was on the 16th or the 17th and the Monastery was taken. I remember that at night when we were shelling the Monastery, you could see the red flashes on the slopes of the hill.

We went back to clean and rest and then we had to go again to Pied de Monte, Route 6. A tank regiment had been sent to go into the small town, but the Germans did not run away but stayed in the town to fight. There were attacks by infantry without result and then my Battalion, the 15th Battalion, got the order to go and help. We were a company of infantry and we went as two sections of Bren Carriers. We waited on Route 6 until it got dark. Then the Germans came with planes and bombed us. A guide led us towards Pied de Monte, but he led us into barbed wire and we had to take the Bren Guns and carry them, leaving the Carriers stranded in the barbed wire. At daylight we moved down the slope to Pied de Monte and here we saw many dead of the Polish forces. We came to some German bunkers and I went into one of them. You had to be careful because of booby traps but I saw a bed and a pillow with something underneath it. It was a wallet full of Italian Lire notes. I took the money and gave the wallet to the Intelligence Officer.

On the left of Route 6 were the Americans and we went in Bren Carriers with orders to reach the final objectives of the 2nd Polish Corps. Near the final objective, which was just a point on the map, we were stopped by the Canadians and told that the Germans were just around the corner with anti tank guns.

For five weeks we were constantly fighting before being finally sent for rest and reorganisation. There were lots of new men who were cooks and clerks, not fighting soldiers. Later, lots of Poles who had been in the German Army joined us. There were many casualties in the rifle companies and there was never time to train the new men properly.

In early July, we moved to the Adriatic coast. Our objective was to cut off Ancona. By this time every Battalion had its own Newssheet and a committee that organised it. Printing had in fact begun while we were in the Middle East. We went by road and up north on the Adriatic coast and we were sent into the hills. In front of us was the 3rd Carpathian Division which we replaced. The idea was to get behind the German defence line, to cut off the town and try not to destroy Ancona so that it could be used as a port by the Allies.

On 3rd July, the platoon leaders were taken to see the ground over which our battalion had got the order to make a night raid. We were taken in lorries to the start line of the raid and from the start line we went through the vines and fields on foot. We had a guide. You attacked two companies up and two behind. I was in front in the right-hand section. There was a lot of tripping on stones and swearing. We came upon an empty and destroyed Sherman tank. Further on, we, and our guide, got lost, but a burning building on the hill helped us find our way. We came upon a little road and as we crossed it, we could see the houses and newly planted fruit trees. We went on and nothing happened. We were within twenty-five yards of a fence with a little gate in it to a garden. The man in front of me bent forward to open the gate and a tracer went up. The man ran and I dived under a stook and called for the PIAT. Nothing happened. I fired a few shots into the fence and then a red sheet opened up in front of me as I was hit by the blast of a German hand grenade.

I found myself lying on my back. When I regained consciousness I could see the moon and it was very silent. I realised that I had been wounded and that I had better get moving and get away. Two years behind barbed wire was enough for me. I sat up and slid down the hill. I expected to be shot in the back and as sliding was too slow, I got up with the help of a tree and started walking. I did not feel any sort of pain. A hundred yards further on I fell through some bushes into woodland and I found my soldiers. A bit of my ear was torn off and my arms and legs were bleeding. They put me into a farm cart and at first they started to take me in the wrong direction straight into the German lines. I ordered them to turn back to our First Aid Post.

Eventually, I got to the Medical point. Someone was talking to me as I opened my eyes and it was our Battalion Medical Officer. By this time, I was beginning to feel the pain and I vaguely remember being put into a jeep and being carried somewhere. The next thing it was dark and I was lying on a stretcher on the ground in a building. It was dark and chilly and I was then carried along empty corridors with footsteps echoing on the stone floors. The door opened into a brightly lit room and there were men in white coats bending over me.

Then there was a beautiful July morning with a blue sky and birds singing. I was lying right by the window. Our Chaplain was giving me the last rites. The next time I opened my eyes, there was an ATS girl sitting beside me. 'Oh you are awake! You are alive. You have been fighting all night!' I was put into an ambulance and taken to a tent at an airfield. It was hot and I was thirsty. There was a lot of dust and there were US Dakota planes landing and taking off. I was eventually put on a plane and flown to Bari and then taken by ambulance to Casa Massina to the Polish Field Hospital. It was now late afternoon. I was put to bed and had a pleasant bed bath after which I slept. I was wounded along my left side, at the top of my ear. Most of my arm, thigh and knee were injured, there was a lucky nick next to my eye and I had a badly mangled foot. There was a lot of talking and arguing amongst the doctors and nurses.

At last a decision was taken and I was returned to my ward. Beside my bed stood a fridge connected to the mains electricity and there was the sister-in-charge with a syringe in her hand. I was told I was getting a course of Penicillin of so many units every two hours for forty-eight hours in a different part of my seat every time. I was also told that as I had lost a lot of blood, I would receive a glass of brandy or sherry with egg yolk each day. Now I was turned face down and suffered very painful injections. Sometimes they put Penicillin powder on to my wounds but I could not sleep because of the shock and I had gangrene in my knee. My leg was full of wood splinters from the German hand grenade and as it was far worse than my head, I was transferred to another ward. My nice nurses would come to see how I was progressing. One of them told me how lucky I was not to lose my leg with gangrene.

While I was in hospital I was given a Commission and I received Officers' pay of £28 a month. I spent six months in hospital and then I was sent to a British camp in Trani for physiotherapy. There I met my friend from the camp in Lithuania. When my wounds would not heal, I went on to a Polish rest camp in tents.

I did not like the camp and I wanted to get back to my Division. One of my friends was going back in a lorry and I went with him. Everything that I possessed was in a gas mask bag. We set out at 5 a.m. and we drove until the late afternoon. It was an open lorry and we had a long, miserable cold drive. I did not know where my battalion was so he dropped me off at the roadside. I was just wondering what to do when a jeep stopped. It was driven by one of the men from the choir in the camp in Lithuania. 'What are you doing here?' he asked. He put me up for the night and the next morning he took me to my unit which was in the line. I waited for my company to come out of the line and I had wine and played cards. There were a lot of new people in the battalion, many of them Poles who had served in the German Army. In my company there were many men from Silesia.

We came back for rest and I was billeted on an Italian family. Then, we moved back to the frontline at the Senio River. There was a railway with a bridge which ran north on the east side of our front and the road to Bologna. There was also a bridge on the west side. Both of the bridges were undamaged and we did not know if they were mined or not. During the day, we slept. There were metal plates on our observation posts. Here we stayed until Easter 1945 when I was told to report to Battalion HQ. 'You are going to England,' I was informed – to the 4th Division which was then being formed.

I went to Rome where I saw an opera which was terrific, and I reported to Naples where I climbed Mount Vesuvius. I then set out on a ship to Liverpool. On the way, we landed in Gibraltar and then we went through some very bad weather, which was not pleasant, in the Irish Sea.

There were crowds of people and bands playing in Liverpool to meet homecoming soldiers. From the boat, we were put on the train to Edinburgh. By that time we knew all about the Yalta agreement and we wondered, 'Where are we going? What are we going to do?' At Carlisle Station, we were given tea with milk in the British style and cakes and sandwiches. From Edinburgh's Caledonian Station, I was sent to Polkemet. I remember it was double summer time and I could not sleep. I remembered the Polar night at Ponoy.

The list arrived with the units and I went to the 1st Grenadiers Battalion in Alyth. In August 1945, we moved to Forres and the Officers' Mess was in Forres Hydro Hotel. Around Christmas 1945, I started learning English. A Polish

Officer serving with the RAF gave me English lessons and a Forres girl who was a student in Edinburgh also taught me English. I remember that I was sent to Keswick for a Bren Carrier Course.

I then joined the Polish Resettlement Corps and I became Adjutant. That winter, we went to Yorkshire to check Artillery ranges for unexploded shells before the land was handed back to the farmers. Those with connections got jobs and I was trying to get to University, but my application was rejected. I tried for University again and when I failed I began looking for courses. I settled on a forestry course and in October 1947 I was sent to Findo Gask Camp to train in forestry, gardening and farming. The course lasted until May 1946. We lived in Nissen huts and I can remember it was very cold.

I was married in April 1948. I remained in Findo Gask on a three-week tractor course and I got a job on Dalkeith Estate while my wife worked at Loretto School. Eventually, in November, I was demobilised in Wiltshire.

I did not think about going back to Poland although my uncle decided to go back. Before he went we agreed a secret code in our letters. I got in contact with my mother who had survived the war and she wrote, 'Stay where you are, do not come here, Uncle Joseph is not very nice to us.'

I almost went to work in East Africa with the Colonial Office, but I did not go as I could not take the family. Instead I got a job, first on an estate in West Lothian, and then on the Winton Estate owned by Sir David Ogilvie where I then became Head Forrester. I worked there until I retired.

Zbigniew Budzyński, 5th Polish Division

Field Kitchen on manoeuvres (© Fife Council Museums East)

Dr Kazimierz Piotr Durkacz
Graduate of the Polish School of
Medicine at The University of
Edinburgh

Edinburgh

At the outbreak of war in 1939, I was a third year Medical Student at Lwów University in the south of Poland, now in the Ukraine. I escaped across the Hungarian border. In Hungary I joined General Maczek and the Free Polish Army.

We went, through Yugoslavia, by railway to France and we trained in the South of France wearing French First World War uniforms and using 1875 French rifles. When the Germans invaded France, we were assigned to part of the defences of Paris. We were taken on trains and then on new American lorries and motorcycles which were issued to us, to the Palace of Versailles, and there, from the cellars, we were issued with new French rifles.

When resistance in France collapsed and Paris was declared an 'Open City', we made our way to near La Rochelle and from here we took a British ship, *Queen Margaret of Scotland*. There were three ships in all and each had 2,000 people aboard. During the retreat from Paris, General Maczek, who was such an efficient soldier, led us and our evacuation was so smooth that we were well ahead of everybody else.

We arrived in Liverpool and we were put on a train to go to Glasgow. I can remember marching up Sauchiehall Street and the welcome that we received in our new uniforms. We were billeted for the first few weeks in Ibrox Stadium in Glasgow.

Hard at work at Johnstone Castle

From there we went to camp in tents in Lanark, Crawford and Biggar. Then, after we had been issued with British uniforms, we went to the East Coast of Scotland, to Arbroath, Forfar, Carnoustie and Broughty Ferry. We were billeted in local houses and we worked on building the coastal defences.

These consisted of large concrete blocks, gun emplacements and observation posts along the shoreline to stop the Germans landing tanks. We were helped in this work by local men. The beaches were also covered with wooden posts and wire.

Dr Kazimierz Piotr Durkacz

At first we just used wood to make the mould for the large concrete blocks and then a combination of corrugated iron and wood. I can remember mixing the concrete with a shovel. Our Polish Squad leaders told us where the lines of blocks were to be placed. The blocks were in double rows along the beaches and the sand dunes and we had to make so many a week. When the concrete had set, the outer case was removed. The gun emplacements were made from blocks with little windows for the guns. We worked in squads of ten men. At that time we were absolutely sure that there would be an invasion and we regularly patrolled the beaches at night.

We also helped the Royal Navy with sea mines. Many mines were washed up on the East Coast and I remember that a lot were washed up on the beach north of Arbroath. Two men from the Royal Navy would come to defuse them and then they would ask us to attach ropes to them and pull them up the beach.

At this time I was learning English by reading the newspapers. I was a private soldier, but by March 1941, I was a Lance Corporal. One day I was given an order to report to Edinburgh. Forty or fifty of us Polish Students had been called up to become the first students of the Polish Medical School of the University of Edinburgh.

We did crash courses in English and continued our Medical studies again. I remember the lectures of Professors Alexander Crew, Sydney Smith, Dunlop and Davidson. I graduated with a MB Ch.B. in 1943 and I stayed on as a lecturer in the Polish Medical School, becoming a specialist in diseases of the mouth.

I could not return to Poland as my home was now in the Soviet Union and I managed to bring my mother to Scotland in 1954. In 1951 I began work at the Edinburgh Dental School and I retired in 1989.

Dr Durkacz was born on the 14th of January 1909. In 2000 he was the last surviving graduate of the Polish Medical School still resident in Edinburgh.

Graduates of the Polish Medical School in Edinburgh 1943

Medical Students of the Polish Medical School

Lieutenant Wiesław Szczygieł
(Lt. Col. George Harvey)
Polish Parachute Brigade

Leven

In August 1939, a few days before the outbreak of the war, as a young twenty year old Regular Army Officer Cadet of the Polish Army Engineers' School, I was posted to my Engineer Regiment in Central South Poland. There I was put in charge of a platoon of reservists being mobilised.

The first days of the war were spent on the organisation and equipment of the unit and then the preparation of the defences of the town.

As the German invasion progressed and the front line troops started withdrawing, my Regimental HQ and the Reserve Depot received orders to evacuate to East Poland where we found ourselves by the 17th September. That was the day the Soviet Army unexpectedly moved into Poland. Not able to fight on two fronts, we received orders to evacuate to Hungary, then a neutral country, and rather sympathetic to Poland. There we were disarmed and interned. The internment was not too strict and there was an organisation run by the Polish Government in Exile in France which facilitated the semi-clandestine evacuation of army personnel to France via Yugoslavia and the still neutral Italy.

I arrived in France in April 1940 and was posted to an Engineer Battalion of the 3rd Polish Division. By then, the 1st and 2nd Divisions were at the front. Our Division was being organised and trained in North West France.

In June, after the fall of France, our battalion evacuated by train to the West of France and eventually boarded the last transport ship available, which, by pure coincidence, happened to be the Polish liner *MS Sobieski*, then under British command.

We arrived at Plymouth on the 22nd June and after a succession of transit camps, our company was deposited on the wet hills near the small town of Crawford in the West of Scotland and ordered to make camp with the bell tents supplied.

The first weeks were rather difficult. Nobody knew the language and there was no news about the war and no news of our country. The Scottish weather did not improve the mood and the British rations, cooked by Polish cooks, were not *haute cuisine*.

Luckily my Engineer Company, being an organised unit, was able to perform engineering tasks common to all army engineers.

So, we were posted to Johnstone in Renfrewshire and later to Lossiemouth in the North of Scotland to build the shore defences.

Another two NCOs, three officers and I were sent to a British Royal Engineers' Company in the Scarborough area to acquaint us with British engineering methods.

At that time, my knowledge of the English language was very limited, but with the help of an English-German dictionary and being left on my own learning English, my improvement was rapid. During the three weeks in Scarborough, my English benefited more than my engineering skills.

This was September 1940, the time of the Battle of Britain, the bombings and the threat of German invasion.

On my return to my company in Scotland, I received the good news that my commission had been verified at last, and as a newly fledged 2nd Lieutenant, I proceeded with the company to another engineering task, building a camp at Tentsmuir for a Polish Battalion which was to defend the eastern shores of the Fife coast and the Leuchars Airfield.

In October 1940, being surplus as an officer in the company, I was posted to the 4th Cadre Rifle Brigade which had newly arrived to defend the south shores of East Fife. This was a unit of some 400 Polish officers and only 100 other ranks. The task of this Cadre Brigade, which was really a battalion, was to man the defences of Fife and patrol the shores. Eventually the unit was to be increased to full strength by Polish volunteers from America.

This did not materialise and our Commanding Officer Colonel Sosabowski (later Major General) had other more ambitious plans. He wanted to form a unit that could eventually be used in the liberation of Poland. So this conglomeration of officers of various ages and professions began to be trained as paratroopers. From early 1941, 'volunteers' were being sent to Ringway, near Manchester, for parachute training by the RAF Para Training School. To speed up the procedure, the preliminary training was done in our own centre in Largo House in Fife where all of the training contraptions were invented and constructed by our engineer officers and a few men.

General Montgomery inspecting Polish paratroopers (© Fife Council Museums East)

By September 1941, we had some 400 Ringway-trained parachutists and in order to receive the recognition of the British and the British authorities, a scheme was organised which included a drop of a company of paratroopers to attack a heavy artillery battery. The exercise was successful and our Prime Minister, General Sikorski, pronounced us, 'The 1st Polish Independent Parachute Brigade'.

By then, the threat of German invasion had passed. We started to receive volunteers from other Polish Units, but mainly from among the men of the 2nd Army Corps evacuated to the Middle East from Soviet Russia.

By 1944, we had almost a full British Army establishment of a Brigade Group consisting of three rifle battalions, an HQ Company, a light artillery battery, an anti tank battery, engineer, signals and medical companies.

This was the time of the Soviet rapid advance in Poland against the retreating Germans, and the Warsaw uprising. Fortunately, or unfortunately, for technical and political reasons, our Brigade could not be used for a drop in Poland.

We were put under British command for use on the second front. In June, the Brigade was transferred to South-East England for final training and equipment and after a few aborted attempts to use us in France, Belgium and Holland, we were dropped at Arnhem in Holland to support the 1st Airborne Division. Unfortunately, due to lack of transport and bad weather, we were dropped too late to be an effective support to the struggling 1st Airborne Division.

The story of that *BridgeToo Far* is well known to all. My story is that I spent three very exciting nights under German fire on the shore of the Neder Rhine with rubber dinghies and wood and canvas assault boats trying to ferry the units of our Brigade to support our British and Polish comrades who were being hammered at Arnhem.[1] After Arnhem, the Brigade spent some time defending bridges and airfields in Holland. We were then transported back to England and after reinforcement and reorganisation, we

---

[1] See Part II *Separated by the Rhine*, page 145

spent time as part of the British Army of the Rhine in Germany.

I left the Brigade to go to the Polish Army Staff School at Peebles after which I was posted to the staff of the 1st Polish Corps in Falkirk which later became the Headquarters of the Polish Resettlement Corps.

On demobilisation in 1948, not being able to return to Poland under the Communist regime, I happily settled in Scotland, married a Scots girl and became a professional photographer.[1]

---

[1] See Part II: Memoirs of Lieutenant W Szczygiel, page 107

Lieutenant Wiesław Szczygieł (Lt. Col. George Harvey)

Field Service with field altar on left (© Fife Council Museums East)

Mrs Elizabeth Kendzia
Ambulance driver with the Fife Voluntary Aid detachment of the Red Cross

Leven

I was born in 1907 and I come from Leven in Fife. Before the Second World War, I studied at The Royal Academy of Dramatic Art after which I taught elocution. I was married and I lived in London. My husband served in the war flying in RAF Lancaster bombers.

My mother, Mrs Reed, was very influential in the Fife Branch of the Voluntary Aid Detachment of the Red Cross and when the Polish Forces arrived in Fife in 1940 and 1941, the Red Cross were urgently looking for local drivers for the Red Cross ambulances to work with the Polish Services. I volunteered.

I was given a smart navy blue uniform and I drove a large motor Field Ambulance with canvas sides. Most of the ambulances were based in Leven and we drove patients who were sick or injured in training between Taymouth Castle and Duplin Castle where the Polish Forces' hospital was based.

I was closely involved in the formation of The Scottish-Polish Society in the area. We organised concerts and drama with the members of the Polish Forces in Leven

Town Hall and we had lots of fun. Having a background in elocution, I also taught English to Polish servicemen and women, all of whom were keen to learn and were eager students. I myself took the opportunity and learnt a little Polish.

As for the Polish men, they were nearly all Officers, very handsome and very attractive to the local girls. I remember at the club on the seafront in Leven, there was one sergeant who used to play the piano most beautifully for the dances and entertainment evenings.

Later in the war after most of the Poles had left Fife for the D-Day landings, a lot of very young Polish recruits arrived – mainly from Silesia. Many of these had been prisoners of the Soviets and only arrived in Scotland towards the end of the war.

When VE Day came, many of the Poles could not go home to Poland, and some simply wanted to make a new life in Scotland. It was very difficult for them and there was a strong local feeling, particularly in the mining community, that they should return to their own country. I remember in particular a meeting in the town hall in Leven by the 'Poles go home' campaigners where strong feelings ran high. I was not proud of my fellow Scots then.

I still have many friends in the surviving members of Scotland's Polish-Scottish community and each year I go to the annual service in Leven and remember those days now so long ago.

Stefan Kwiatkowski
1st Lieutenant Polish Army
(by Stefan G Kay OBE, assisted by Barbara E Kay)

Penicuik

S tefan Kwiatkowski was the eldest son of the family, born in Socołovo near Ostrołęka in the Russian zone of Poland in December 1908. His father, a builder as well as farmer, had to pack his belongings and the family into a farm cart, and go to work for the Russian Army in the Eastern Campaigns of the Great War. One of my father's vivid memories of Kiev was seeing the Cossacks ride down with drawn sabres on a crowd supporting the Bolshevik Revolution – it interrupted the journey to school! When the Russians withdrew from the conflict, the family had to make the long trudge back to Poland and rebuild the farm.

Educated in Law at Warsaw University, he supported himself by working for a major bank, and became an Army Reservist, with the rank of 2nd Lieutenant at the outbreak of war in 1939. His unit was sent south immediately. 'Leave the Regulars to do what they can against the invaders' was the order, and, with some good fortune evading German forces, he made it to Romania where he was interned, but treated comparatively kindly.

With the help of the Polish authorities and the French Embassy, using his mother's name and with his military documents concealed in the sole of his boots, he made it out of Romania, across Italy before that country joined Germany at war, and rejoined the Polish Army as it reformed near Paris. My father remembered that winter of 1939/40 as bitterly cold, being constantly hungry, waiting for the Germans to come and worrying about his family – with good reason. Although most of the family survived the war, his sister Genka was caught and put to death by the Germans in 1944. She had worked for the Resistance throughout.

The 1940 invasion of France, and the evacuation from Dunkirk, still left a lot of Allied soldiers and adherents in France less than willing to wait to be captured without hitting back at the enemy. My father was part of a motorised convoy which made its way South, collecting military personnel and families on the way. One alternative was to cross the Spanish border into certain and less than hospitable internment in Fascist Spain; another, knowing that British and Allied ships were still making pick-ups along the Atlantic coast, was to try to find a ship to get away from France.

The convoy was as far as Les Sables d'Olonne, before they were advised that they might be picked up at La Rochelle by a British vessel. The *Ullapool* indeed came into the harbour and picked up as many people as it could handle. They went aboard with the clothes they wore and the hand weapons they could carry, but not before leaving spiked guns and disabled vehicles to deny their use to the approaching Germans.

Lt John White RNR (on right) on *HMS Maid Marion* in 1941. He was part of the convoy which brought Stefan Kwiatkowski to the UK

Joining a convoy well out into the Atlantic, my father landed in Plymouth on 20th June 1940. Among the naval ships escorting the convoy was the salvage vessel *Maid Marion* commanded by my great-uncle Lt John White RNR, who was later to meet my father in Scotland

From Plymouth, the tired soldiers were sent North by train. My father said that every station seemed to be called 'Gentlemen' – pronounced in a Polish way – as of course station name boards had all been taken down to confuse an invader and, no doubt, local travellers too! They were encamped near Biggar and slowly reformed into units.

My maternal grandfather, George S Taylor – the first volunteer for the Home Guard in Peebles – was a dentist in that town, and spotted what he thought were French troops when on his way to Lanark to see a friend. He was told that they were in fact Poles, but had been equipped with French uniforms in France before the German invasion.

A hospitable family, my grandparents soon invited some of the Polish refugees in Peebles into their home. One day, my father, visiting a friend, came along too and soon made his mark with my mother, then just seventeen, and they started to correspond and he visited as often as he could.

Sent to create and man defences along the Fife coast, Stefan became part of the 1st Polish Independent Parachute Brigade, part of the 1st Airborne Division, training as a paratrooper – and breaking an ankle, at Manchester Ringway Airport.

Promoted 1st Lieutenant just before his marriage, Stefan married Barbara Elizabeth Taylor in Peebles on 14th October 1943 in St Joseph's Church with the Polish

Chaplain, Father Mientki SJ, and the local parish priest, Father James Harold, officiating. Wartime rules applied so that there were only forty guests allowed, and larders were scoured to produce a wedding breakfast. It is worth noting that even in those less ecumenical days – my grandparents were Episcopalian – that the congregation represented all the Christian faiths of Peebles.

14th October 1943: wedding at St Joseph's Church, Peebles. Zygmunt Krasinski on right and behind him Dr Zborowski

He then went into training for Arnhem, by which time I was expected. As Supply Officer, he was dropped by parachute on the South side of the Rhine near Driel, with instructions to hold the position to allow the earlier troops, who had taken awful punishment from the Germans, to escape across the river. Posted missing, he phoned my mother three weeks later from Stamford, having made his way back to Allied lines. He was the only one of the eight Supply Officers to survive Arnhem.

On VE Day, 8th May 1945, he was posted to the Army of Occupation in Germany where he was a Presiding Officer at Courts Martial – a job he hated – and then in the same role in the Resettlement Corps at Polkemmet, West Lothian (where my mother and I lodged). I can just remember this at the age of three! During this period, he was promoted to Staff Captain and given a British Commission.

Discharged from the Army in 1948, and having decided that to return to a Communist Poland was not for him, Stefan sought work – he could not return to the Law without a conversion course at Edinburgh University which could not be afforded. He was right about not going back for fear of retribution. My godfather, Captain Count Zygmunt Krasiński, went back, was imprisoned for his pains and was only allowed, when finally released, to do quite menial jobs. I met him in Krakow in 1965: a humorous, slightly sardonic man. He played a mean mouth organ, I am told!

However, one thing Poles rarely lack is an ability to work, especially if family needs are to be met, so, helped by kindly references from friends in Peebles, Stefan found employment in the office at the paper mills of Alex Cowan & Sons Ltd in Penicuik – an industry to which I too was to devote most of my working life. He also took British nationality and changed his name from Kwiatkowski to Kay, having checked that this was not an uncommon name in Scotland if you include the Kaye and Keay variants!

I am sure that there were, from time to time, incidents which could be classed as resentment or prejudice against my father, but these were rarely to his face. For quite a small man, he was both fit and powerful. My mother recalls one incident when some dirt was put into my pram as a baby, but this was after a Pole, locally, much disturbed by his war injuries, had murdered his Scottish wife.

The paper mill gave us a little house in Bridge Street in Penicuik in 1951 which took me away from my beloved Peebles, and my younger sister, Anne, arrived not too long afterwards. That let Stefan and Barbara have their own home at long last, after eight years of marriage and living with the in-laws. In 1953, we were proud to get the keys of a three-bedroom council house in Woodside Drive, which was to be the Kay home for over forty years.

That, along with access to normal education at school, and then university level for my sister and me, could hardly be said to constitute discrimination. Apart from some teasing about my name at school, I can honestly say that I never felt prejudice against me. We were, of course, living in small country towns with small Polish populations.

My father retrained as a Chartered Secretary and stayed at the paper mill until the mill closed in 1972. (For five years, he and I worked in the same industry.) He had taken up part-time accountancy work, and the advent of VAT coincided with being made redundant to his great benefit as he worked for many of the businesses in Penicuik putting in their VAT systems.

He played a full part in the British Legion and in the Polish Paratroopers' Association. Contacts with Poland were difficult until things thawed and my paternal grandmother, 'Babcia', was able to visit us in 1961. This was a great day for the family. She was horrified that the crop of mushrooms in the nearby woods was not being harvested by the Scots! Before then, we came home from church one extremely wet Sunday morning in December 1958 to find my cousin Janek on the doorstep. A survivor of the concentration camps and the forced labour gangs, he was then dealing in postage stamps, and 'stamp soup' in the bath as they were soaked off their envelopes to be dried and sorted is a memory. I had a great collection of Polish stamps, however!

We went as a family to Poland on holiday in July 1965. To be met at the station by so many relatives was a very emotional moment for us all. My 21st birthday party was in Warsaw. I am told that there was a major thunderstorm in the early hours of the morning, but the combination of Scotch, vodka and food did not keep me awake.

Further visits by my father to Poland were to follow, the last when he was some eighty years of age. He spoke on Polish Radio about his wartime experiences and his Army uniform resides in his old school in Ostrołeka. He only fully retired at seventy-five when my mother retired from her job as School Administrator at St David's High School in Dalkeith. He gained great pleasure from visiting his family around the country and took pride in his grandchildren.

An active man all his life, he died in 1997 after a very short illness, and is buried – with quite a few of his compatriots – in Penicuik, a long distance in miles and years from Poland.

POSTSCRIPT

Life moves in strange ways. I have been almost a lifelong steam railway enthusiast and 1997, and every year since, has taken me to the little town of Wolsztyn, about fifty miles from Poznań, there to be a trainee steam locomotive driver. Driving the 0507 commuter train to Poznań, under the careful eye of the professional crew, is quite an experience and tests my very limited command of the language to its limits. Both my daughters, Catherine and Rosie, and my niece Stefanie, have been out to Poland to work on Polish steam too. I am told that we all fit quite naturally into the scene there.

Our second daughter, Rosie, trained as a contemporary ballet dancer in London, and on graduation in 1998, took up a position with Polski Teatr Tanca in Poznań which she held until early in 2000. She has many friends in Poland.

The connections between Poland and Scotland are very much alive!

Stefan Kay Junior

**Summer 1942 in Lundin Links. Kneeling: Władek Dobrowolski.
Standing (left to right): Alek Pronobis; Miss Turnbull (landlady);
Zygmunt Krasinski; Barbara Taylor and Stefan Kwiatkowski**

Lieutenant Colonel J J Korabiowski
4th Polish Infantry Division

Glenrothes

I was born on 5th March 1909 in the south of Poland, an area that is now part of the Ukraine. I started work in the town's Technical Department after gaining my General Certificate of Education (GCE). In the spring of 1928, I enrolled to do National Service; then on the 16th July, I was called to the Officer's School of the Artillery Reserve. After completing my training, I was sent to the 5th Field Artillery Regiment (FAR) in Lwów to complete my National Service (a total of fifteen months). I then enlisted as a regular soldier and when I successfully passed all the tests, I was accepted into the School for Artillery Officers in Toruń. Two years later, I was promoted to 2nd Lieutenant and attached to the 11th FAR where I was given the duties of a junior officer to the 8th Battery. This Battery had 100mm howitzers driven by horses. Each year, new recruits were trained on range practice and infantry manoeuvres. In January 1934, I was promoted to Lieutenant, then in 1939, to Captain. Throughout this time I served with the 11th Carpathian FAR.

Mobilisation went smoothly according to plan and by the third day, the Battery was moving west by rail. The transport was occasionally interrupted by attacks from the

German air force which were fended off by the Battery's machine guns. On the morning of the second day, the Battery was given orders to disembark at a small station which only had room for two wagons; hence it involved a lot of manoeuvring to unload the heavy equipment. At great risk, the horses jumped from the wagons without injuries. The Battery then took up position two kilometres from the station in a large orchard where it was attacked by eight German bombers; the attack was fought off with machine guns and hand held guns. Thankfully, this time, there were no casualties. After feeding men and horses, the Battery marched on, covering itself over wide gaps. By evening, it had joined up with two other batteries; all three were under one commanding officer.

The next day, defensive positions were taken up by the Battery and the infantry units, shooting throughout at the Germans who were attacking rather indecisively. After a night and a day in this position, there was a long and tiring march east while being attacked from the air and by occasional small groups of tanks which our cannons successfully fought off. Two days and nights later, we took up a defensive position fighting battles with advancing Germans. Tanks attacked the Horse Transport Division at the rear of this defensive position but these were destroyed by a neighbouring battery. We marched again two nights later with frequent gun action, the division taking up a 'hedgehog' formation so as to defend itself from all angles and so as not to be outstripped by the German motorized forces. Battles were now more frequent.

As the three infantry battalions and the three batteries that had covered the disembarkation of the division at the station had been seized by the army at Kraków, the division only had part of its battalion and battery from that point onwards.

It became a custom to march through the night and take up a defensive formation through the day. Near the locality of 'K', a heavy battle raged all day; we felt the force of the German artillery whilst the German infantry suffered greatly from ours. With the coming of night, we removed ourselves from the enemy while a few batteries were still firing at the preceding units. During this night march it was discovered that the enemy had fortified a section of the route, a problem which was resolved by one of the infantry battalions.

By morning, we reached the large town of Przemyśl where our maps ended. Our march continued until we reached a small village beyond Przemyśl where we stopped for a longer rest, restocking on ammunition and supplies at a nearby railway station. Again, in the night, we marched. Tiredness was noticeable in both men and horses. Progress was at two kilometres per hour. The roads were crowded with supply wagons pulled by horses. After the march, the Battery rested in a wooded area. The sky was constantly full of German planes. In the evening, after successfully gaining a German position, the infantry unit reorganised and marched on. In a further skirmish, the entire SS German Brigade was defeated; it was made up of three battalions, artillery and tanks, and was assisted by the reconnaissance unit of a neighbouring division. SS Germania, as the Brigade was called, was never rebuilt. Then, at the start of the day, the Battery destroyed a tank that appeared in the morning mist.

We entered the woods where the battle continued for a further two days and one night. The Battery now had six guns having gained another two when the 4th Battery, which had stayed in Przemyśl to strengthen its defences joined it. During the night we broke away from the Germans. The 5th and 6th Batteries marched with a small company of infantry. The road was difficult, narrow and sandy. At the exit to the wood, it was discovered that the Germans surrounded the area so it was decided to force our way through. A minimum number of men stayed with the horses; the rest fixed bayonets and prepared for battle, the infantry on our left flank. We approached the Germans as quietly as possible and attacked. Surprised and stunned, the Germans willingly surrendered. There were about 200 of them. From our prisoners we learnt that they had arrived in the afternoon and had set up their defences with their backs to the wood. We had attacked their rear. In this manoeuvre we had only sustained one casualty.

The Battery then marched through the day, being continually dissected by enemy air attacks. In the evening, it was joined by a further two guns from the 4th Battery on the outskirts of a large town. The commanding officer of the 4th Battery had died in the hospital at Przemyśl from severe wounds. The next day, the 4th Battery was reformed but the following day its new commanding officer was killed by tanks in battle. The remaining three guns of the 4th Battery joined the 5th Battery. A further two guns from the 3rd

Battery joined the 5th giving it a total of nine guns. There was no shortage of ammunition as the garrison's ammunition depot at Lwów was close by. However, a secure passage to Lwów was not successful despite four infantry encounters of the whole Karpaty Army of about 1,500 infantry. In the first attack, 100 men got through the German position but the gap was destroyed by the onslaught of tanks. The Germans had a well-organised defence position with a good machine gun section. Later in the day, a group of tanks attacked the 5th Battery position from the rear, but lost five tanks and retreated. Throughout the night, I was in the observation point in the first line of the infantry and witnessed the Germans retreat and then in the morning saw the Soviet Army advancing. We were taken captive by the Soviets. Thankfully, that evening, I escaped at dusk.

In Lwów, realising that I could not get back to my garrison as it was occupied by the Soviets, I changed into civilian clothing and headed west, leaving my wife and infant son behind. I managed to cross the German Soviet line safely and after two days walking, I reached the Slavonic border. The local leader of smugglers gave me a map and information on how to reach the Hungarian border. I also acquired some dressings for my festering leg wound and left Poland. After four days of minor events, I reached the shelter at Erika in Hungary. Here, there were three soldiers; one took me to the village where the entire platoon was positioned and the next day I was escorted to another place to be handed over to the military police. I was then sent by rail to Koszyc into the care of the army. From there, the next day, I was sent to the Internment Camp at Hidas Nemeti.

After four weeks, I left on an evening train to arrive in
Budapest in the early afternoon where I reported to the
Polish Embassy. A few days later, with a false passport, I
travelled to France. After verification, I was sent on a four-
week course run by French Officers' Battery Command
which only covered the ABC of the artillery. Once the
course was completed, I was made the commander of the 4th
Battery in the 2nd FAR.

My second-in-command and I had to fight many
hardships. The Battery consisted of one hundred and twenty-
five men. We had four guns, twenty-five rifles (long
barrelled), two heavy machine guns, two hand-held machine
guns and several revolvers, all from the previous war. Thus
we went into battle. Our worst problem was that of
communication as we only had one patrol phone with a four-
kilometre cable. The Battery eventually received its horses
five days before it set off by rail. However, the Battery
lacked qualified riders whilst the horses were thin and had
various wounds and flees. On arrival in the area of Nancy,
behind the Maginot Line, I gave lessons in horse riding,
driving horses in harness and field service.

Four weeks later, the Battery was moved to the
stronghold of Belfort. Then, a few days later, without having
fired a shot, the Battery was on the march south. On the
march, many hardships were encountered with the route
being blocked by fleeing civilians and soldiers. Our 2nd DSP
(2nd Fusiliers Division) joined the 45th French Corps, which
still had two French divisions. These divisions were already
split. The skies over the next few days, were full of Italian
planes. The Battery took up a firing position, returning

several rounds, mainly against tanks. During such manoeuvres we neared the Swiss border and shielded French soldiers crossing it. After more rounds of fire and the change of some positions, the Battery, with the barrels of our guns still warm, crossed into Switzerland. At the border, the division commander accepted my report on the action and the state of the Battery: no losses and no wounded.

In Switzerland, the Battery, following several moves, was housed in the village of Pfafnau. I remained with my Battery men whilst the younger officers were sent to studies organised at the University. The following year, we were moved to Matzinger and at the end of that year, to Sarnen. The stance of the Swiss changed with the changes on the Soviet/German front: they stopped fearing the Germans. This resulted in a secret agreement to run Polish Army courses. I was then moved to a camp in Pfaffikon as an artillery instructor on such secret courses.

In the summer of 1944, I received orders to return to France to support the underground FF1 by recruiting Polish soldiers. The intention was to rebuild the 2nd DSP in France once the Germans had left. At the end of September 1944, this project was cancelled. At this time, I had 800 men under my command and several Swiss border crossing points. I received orders that the men of the 2nd DSP were to be sent to Great Britain and the rest to the 2nd Corps. For a while I was in a camp in Sorgues near Avignon where the Americans brought Poles from the Wehrmacht. I sent these in groups of 600 men to Marseille to be put on ships for Italy.

I came to Britain in January 1945. First I was on a short course in Dalkeith before being was transferred to 14 FAR (4DP) in Selkirk. In August 1945, I was promoted to Major. The regiment passed all the tests and was qualified for action but during this time the war ended. Occupation was discussed and it was proposed to join the PRC (Polish Resettlement Corps) and organise trips back to Poland and other countries. My last function was Chief of the Welfare Committee and Chief of Liquidation of Polish Camps.

In May 1949, I was demobbed and worked as a bus conductor, and later as a driver in Wolverhampton. However, my earnings were low for my needs as I still had a wife, son and mother to support in Poland. My wife was in greatest need as she had lost her sight due to injuries sustained during the war. I moved to Scotland to work in the construction of tunnels for Hydro Electric. The shifts were long: twelve hours rotating from day to night shift and living on campus. Although I had started work with pick and shovel, I ended up as a foreman. This work gave me the opportunity to save enough to bring my wife and son over from Poland via Austria in the autumn of 1956.

Being reunited with my wife after seventeen years was very emotional for us both despite being in touch by mail (although I had to write under an alias). I had left behind a nineteen-year-old woman with a baby and met a thirty-six-year-old in dark glasses. When I asked her to remove them, I saw deep sockets where once were bright eyes.

My son was aiming at his GCEs and had been accepted for studies at university. To be closer to the family,

I changed jobs and worked for the Coal Board, and, as time passed, so did the family increase with the arrival of a second son and then a daughter while the oldest son married.

Prior to the war, I had graduated from the Polish Academy of Physical Education and my wife managed to bring me my certificates. However, I was unsuccessful at getting a teaching job in Scotland on the grounds that I was not a British Citizen and because of my religion.

Since the death of my wife in 1995, I live on my own and continue doing my best to be a useful citizen and to promote Polish culture within my strength and abilities.

Lt Col J J Korabiowski

Squadron Leader Lesław Międzybrodzki AFC RAF

Edinburgh

In 1939 I was twenty-seven years old and living in Kraków. I had just finished Technical University in Lwów and I still had to do National Service. I got a temporary job in a maintenance unit of the Air Force.

On 31st August, I was in charge of the night shift when I received a telephone call from Civil Defence stating that as lights were showing from the hangers we were to stop work. Everybody went home. I was woken up by the sound of aircraft, but these were not Polish aircraft; they were German. The hangers were destroyed in an air raid. Fortunately, our aircraft had been moved to the field landing strip.

Returning to the base, we received word that we were moving to Lwów. In three days we packed everything, all the equipment and aircraft spares that we could carry, and set off in a convoy of lorries and started driving towards Lwów. We arrived on 3rd or 4th September 1939 and we started unpacking. We then got orders to pack up again and go further east. We reached the Romanian frontier and we stayed on the Polish side until the 17th of September when an

Army Captain arrived on a motorbike and told me that the Russians had invaded Poland.

I decided that the only sensible thing to do was to cross the border into Romania. We got to Tulcea in Bessarabia and we were taken to an internment camp.

We were going to be interned in Babadak, quite a dreadful place. On the way there I saw, in the middle of the street, my best friend. We had attended the same university, we had gone skiing together and at one time we shared digs together instead of staying in the camp in Lwów.

We decided to go on our own to Bucharest. I had been paid three months salary before we left Poland, and because I had been able to change the money on the way, I had plenty of it.

We got to Bucharest and we went to the Polish Legation where we said that we wanted to volunteer for the Polish Air Force. After obtaining passports and visas we then went by train to Belgrade and visited the Polish Air Attaché. He stamped 'Aviation' in our passports and sent us on our way to France.

As we wanted to see Venice and the Alps, we took about a week going through Italy, travelling through Milan, Venice and Turin. It was a very pleasant journey and the Italians were very friendly and anti-German, encouraging us on the border by shouting '*Aviatori Polenaise*' to us,

We reached the French frontier and we received our first shock when we saw the poor state of the French Army. We really did not want to believe that they were as bad as they were, but even at the frontier post, we could see that they did not have much chance of winning the war.

Finally, we reached Paris and we went to find the Polish Air Attaché. When we got to the Polish Air Force Headquarters we were told that it would take some time before we could start our flying training and that we should finish Officer School before going into the Air Force.

When the Germans attacked France in 1940, we had just finished Officer School, but there was still a problem getting into the Air Force. As France fell, we made our way with the Army to St Jean de Luz where we got away on the Polish Liner *Sobieski*. On the way to the ship we passed through an area where the British Army had retreated from their positions. Here we found a machine gun and some ammunition which we took with us and we mounted the gun on the upper deck of the ship as air defence.

We arrived at Plymouth and there we were put on a train. I was impressed with what I saw. I still had some French money and when the people in the carriage started playing poker, I won quite a lot of French francs which I later managed to change.

The journey ended at Aintree racecourse where we were put into tents. Later we went to RAF Kirby and to Blackpool. We met many others who also wanted to fly. A Polish Air Squadron, 302 Squadron, was being formed and I was posted as ground staff. We were told that we would get on a flying course when training started. Others were sent to a second Polish Squadron, 303 Squadron. I felt very lucky being involved and having something to do, but there was still a problem getting into Flying School.

The Squadron moved to RAF Leconfield and during the Battle of Britain a detachment of the Squadron was sent to RAF Duxford, near Cambridge. I was with that detachment as ground staff and the Squadron had many successes. In 303 Squadron, some of those like me who wanted to do flying training went on hunger strike and stopped going to the Mess, protesting that they wanted to fly.

Finally, in 1941, I was posted to Flying School. Some of the ground training was in London and it was here that I first saw cricket at Lords Cricket Ground where we had some of our lectures. I trained on Tiger Moths at RAF Huckwal and on Oxfords at RAF Newton where I got my pilot's wings. At that time, there was an over production of pilots and twenty of us were posted to RAF Morpeth to fly Lysanders and Bothas. Half of those who flew the Bothas were killed. Part of it was bad luck; part of it was bad aircraft.

I was posted to Coastal Command and went on a general reconnaissance course and then to an Operational Training Unit (OTU) where I started flying as a second pilot. After six operational flights in 304 Squadron, instead of the usual thirty flights, I was posted and got my own crew. As my first pilot was an ex-Lot Polish Airlines' pilot, he and I were mistaken for one another and the rumour went around that I had had experience with LOT and men came to me and asked if they could fly with me. Later, one of these men noticed my logbook and saw that I had only 400 hours flying. He was very disappointed.

I flew Wellington Mark 14s out of Davidstow Moor, Predannack in Cornwall, Chivenor in Devon and Benbecula.

Coastal Command flying was very boring. We flew for ten to eleven hours at fifty feet above the sea at night,

night after night, looking for U-Boats. Sometimes you were virtually falling asleep. Most never saw a U-Boat. However, I saw three and have attacked two. This was in the Bay of Biscay. Two U-Boats were on the surface at night recharging their batteries. The moonlight was very bright and I saw them clearly. I gave the order to switch on the Leigh light and we went into the attack. As soon as the U-boats saw the Leigh light they started firing at us. The idea was that you flew over the U-Boat at an angle and dropped a depth charge on either side of the submarine. The problem was that we flew over the first submarine and dropped our depth charges and we then had to fly over the second submarine. In the process, our wing was badly hit by the enemy fire of the second submarine and I lost control of the aircraft for a brief time.

When daylight came, we could see the size of the hole in our aircraft, but we had sunk one submarine and we got home.[1]

I was on Benbecula for six weeks flying Wellington Bombers Mark 14 while patrolling the northern sea approaches north of Benbecula. It was November. We were living in Nissen huts. The nights were long and we had problems with the wind, sheep on the runway and the mice eating our woollen uniforms which we had to hang from string, attached to the ceiling. We did not have very much contact with the local people, but when we went to get our washing done by the locals, there was great difficulty because they were Gaelic speakers.

---

[1] *The Bay of Biscay*, page 149

I always had an ambition to combine engineering with test flying and a chance meeting in the Mess resulted in my being posted to The Armament and Aircraft Experimental Establishment at Boscombe Down where I spent many years having an interesting and pleasant time doing just that. There were about ten other members of the Polish Air Force at Boscombe Down at the time.

My last posting was to Farnborough and in 1947/48 when the war was over I was offered a permanent commission in the Royal Air Force where I stayed until 1961 testing all sorts of aircraft, including modern British and American jets. During the war I was awarded the Polish Virtuti Militari and after the war, the Air Force Cross.

I had to retire from the Royal Air Force at the age of forty-nine and by chance I met a man at Farnborough Air Show who asked me to join Ferranti to do more flying and testing. There were about forty or fifty other Poles who also worked at Ferranti. I finally retired from Ferranti in 1983.

After the war, I managed to get my mother to the United Kingdom. My brother was a shipbuilding engineer. On the outbreak of war he was working on the Baltic and went with the Polish Navy to a place called Hel, in the Gulf of Danzig, which was the last place in Poland to capitulate to the Germans. Contrary to the terms of surrender, when he should have been sent to an *Oflag* or *Stalag* as a Prisoner of War or sent home as a civilian, he spent the war in Stutrov and Sachsenhausen Concentration Camps. After the war he came to the west through Sweden and he settled in Canada.

– October 2000

Squadron Leader Międzybrodzki died on Thursday 18th January 2001. I shall remember him a charmingly modest man with a wry sense of humour whose flying log books of the early Cold War period made quite remarkable reading. He had flown and tested virtually every operational aircraft of the period, many of them secret.

His exploit in the Bay of Biscay is more fully recorded in and extract from '*Destiny Can Wait – The History of The Polish Air Force Association in Great Britain.*' See extract on page 149.

**Polish Officers at the RAF Air Experimental Establishment,
Boscombe Down 1945-1946**

**Left to right: Flt lt Międzybrodzki, Sqn Ldr Zurakowski, Air Comdr
Fraser RAF, Sqn Ldr Preiss, Sqn Ldr Kulczycki, Flt Lt Pegulski**

Lech S Muszyński
Aged eleven at the time of the outbreak
of the Second World War

Leven

I was born on 11th December 1928 in Osada Wolawel
District Drohiczyn, Wojwodship Polesie, Poland. My
father, Stanisław Mucha-Muszyński, joined the Polish
Legion led by the then commandant, Jósef Piłsudski, in
1914. He took part in most of the battles, including the Battle
of Warsaw in August of 1929, also known as 'The Miracle
of Vistula'. For his distinguished service, he and many
others, were given land in the Eastern part of Poland. They
were called The Military Settlers. He was much decorated,
his decorations including the Virtuti Militari Class 5, the
Cross of Valour and the Polish Cross of Independence.

At the beginning of the Second World War, on 18th
September 1939, my father joined the retreating Polish
Division, making his way to Hungary with a view to fighting
the Germans and the Russians while awaiting France and
Britain to attack Germany from the West. This did not
materialise. My mother, sister and I were left in the corridor
between the two advancing fronts. Ukrainian and Belarus
gangs constantly harassed The Military Settlers by killing
some of them and robbing the rest of everything they could

lay their hands on. Eventually, the Soviet Army occupied that part of Poland, and put a stop to most of the killings, but the robberies went on.

On 10th February 1940 at 3 a.m. we were awakened by loud banging on the door and the barking of our dogs. We were given half an hour to get ready: '*Sobierajtsie z wieshchami*', one Mongolian looking Russian soldier hurried us terribly. We were loaded onto a sled. It was very cold. Another Russian soldier ran back into the house, and came out with his arms full of warm bedding. Covering us, he said, 'You will need it where you are going.'

We were taken to our school where all the rest of the Military Settlers' families were assembled. From there we were loaded, fifty to a railway cattle truck, with wooden boards one above the other as living and sleeping accommodation. In the middle there was a stove and a hole in the floor as a toilet. There were two small windows above the bunks diagonally with steel bars. That morning, 10th February 1940, our journey into the unknown began.

The conditions in our truck were horrendous: no privacy at the toilet; no water whatever; women with small babies; old men and children crammed together and white frost on the walls and ceiling to which our hair and skin stuck. February 1940 was a very cold month with minus 40° temperatures. Two days later, we were shunted to some sidetracks, given coke for the stove, some hot soup, hot water, and some bread. There were other transports in the sidings, as we could hear men's voices shouting in unison, 'bread and water'. They were Polish Prisoners of War.

After three weeks of this inhuman journey, we arrived at our destination. Lesopunkt, Nuchto Ozero, Jemca District, Archangel Region, Northern Siberia, Soviet Union. We were herded in to communal barracks, eighty people to each. There was one large wood-burning stove in the middle; each family was given wooden bunks for children, wooden frames for adults, a small table, one bench and a little room for luggage. Next day our labour camp Commandant spoke to us. He told us to work hard for the glory of the Soviet Union, and to stop thinking of ever going back to Poland and our homes, and said:

'Kak swinia nie zobachit nieba tak vy svoiei Polshy.'
('As a pig will never see Heaven, neither you will see your Poland again.')

Other NKVD staff told us of our rights: we had none. They informed us of the allocation of bread and soup to workers who fulfilled their quotas of work. Those who failed their quotas and the sick would receive half ration, children up to age fourteen would also receive half ration but they must attend the local school.

Mother was allocated work at a steam driven sawmill producing railway sleepers. Her work was to carry away all the off-cuts from below the saw, and stack them up a good distance away. Her immediate superior was an old Ukrainian tyrant, himself a deportee in Stalin's clearances of 1933. Her work was far too heavy; she could not fulfil her quota, and, as a result, her food ration was reduced by half.

In the meantime, we had a terrible problem with bed bug infestation, there were no washing facilities, the holes in the ground as toilets were frozen and there was a general lack of hygiene facilities. After numerous complaints, the camp authorities sent a district hygiene inspector to talk to us. She told us to use steam baths previously reserved for the labour camp staff, and the previous deportees. She also told us that the Soviet Union had the highest culture and hygiene in the world. As an example, she quoted that each District had at least 'one hundred *Voshoboikas*' – delousing houses.

By now I was attending school. For the first few weeks we were taught nothing else but the Russian language. It was easy to learn as it is very similar to Belarus and most of us understood it. Then a new teacher started coming for the first hour each morning, asking a lot of questions about what our adults were talking about, but knowing that she was a Political Commissar, we never answered her and sat like dummies. She was very cross and used to call us a lot of names, until, instead of her, an NKVD woman in uniform and carrying a stick started to come to our class. She was huge with bulging eyes that got bigger as she got angry. We called her '*Wiedzma*' – a witch. She told us stories about the successes of the Soviet Union and its heroes. She used to take great delight in asking the local boys, who were already indoctrinated and did not know any differently, to tell us about the heroes of the Soviet Union – Lenin, Stalin, Woroshilow, Chkalow and others. We were sure that she had been sent in to intimidate us with her size and the stick that she always carried.

One morning she was in a good mood. She gave each of us a sweet and said that she was going to tell us about a man who is a father to all the children, not only in Russia, but everywhere. She said, 'Those who know stand up!' and all the locals did. She gave them a sweet each and sent then out to play for the rest of the hour. She said to us, 'There is a man living in the Kremlin in Moscow who loves all the children like his own, and Polish children should learn to love him back as he loves them. His name is Stalin.' One eleven year old Polish boy, the son of a Polish forester named Halinski, stood up and said to her, 'If Stalin loves us so much, then what are we and our families doing here, suffering such terrible hardship, and when is he going to send us back home to Poland?'

She started screaming that our fathers and mothers were capitalist bloodsuckers, the enemies of the Soviet Union and all the workers of the world. She stormed out and returned with a Deputy Camp Commandant who dismissed us for the rest of the day, our fate being decided by his superior. The next morning we were told that as a punishment we were being sent to burn branches in the forest. The work was hard but we enjoyed the company of older men who told us that we were worthy sons of Polish Military Settlers.

Spring comes late to Siberia, but when it comes, it is very sudden. Days get very long and warm. Snow, ice and soil thaw down to the perma-frost. All the rebel boys were released from work in the forest to clear and cultivate a piece of ground. Each family was allocated a piece. Ours was forty by thirty metres of virgin Siberian land full of tree stumps which my sister Irena helped to clear and plant with potatoes and vegetable seeds given to us free by the camp authorities. My mother and many other people developed dusk blindness and slack teeth due to lack of vitamins in our meagre diet.

Summer in the Siberian tundra and taiga is a time of plenty if you know your wild berries and mushrooms. I acquired some empty salt herring barrels and we proceeded to salt certain kinds of mushrooms, preserve blueberries, huckleberries and others, which, together with the amazing crop of potatoes and vegetables from out plot, helped to restore mother's health and also helped to sustain us through the next winter. Mother was given lighter work and Irena started work as a nanny to the camp baker. Life was getting better. We were told to return to school. After a few days we were sent to a corrective camp twenty kilometres away because we called our old friend the witch stupid and brainless for trying to tell us that, 'if ever anything happened to Stalin, then the sun would never rise again.'

In the autumn of 1940, the old Commandant was replaced by a young 2nd Lt NKVD. The old one went for medical treatment to Moscow which meant only one thing. The new Commandant got our release and we rejoined our families. He taught our people how to cheat to attain their respective quotas in the forest industry; this meant that everybody qualified for full rations of food, and my mother and sister were paid a little money after a 10% deduction for the upkeep of the camp. He also got some warm clothing called 'fufajka' and felt boots, 'walonki'. We all survived the winter of 1940/41, except for a few old people, thanks to him.

After Germany's attack on their ally, the Soviet Union, in June 1941, our Government in exile in Britain led by General Wladyslaw Sikorski signed a treaty with the Soviet Union releasing all Polish nationals from prisons, POW camps and labour camps, and on 12th August 1941, we were free. The Polish Army was being formed in the Southern Soviet Republic, and that was where we decided to go. My mother said Polish soldiers would help women and children survive.

We knew that the journey south was going to be very long and a journey to the unknown. We harvested our second crop from our plot, dried some bread, and waited for our transport to be allocated to us by Soviet authorities. As our food was dwindling, we finally boarded cattle trucks again (this time open and without steel bars on the windows). On 11th November 1941, approximately 750 people set out on an epic journey south, during which there was a lot of suffering due to starvation, diseases and long delays on the railway sidings with priority being given to Russian Army and civilian requirements. Our food and money ran out, an epidemic of typhus was decimating our dwindling numbers. At last, on Christmas Day 1941, we arrived in Buchara. At our destination 420 had survived.

After working on a nearby cotton growing Collective Farm, we met with more starvation and illness. We went back to Bukhara where my sister and I joined the Polish Army as young soldiers. I was posted to the 7th Division in Kermine (Navoi), and Irena joined a Polish Girls' Unit in Guzar. Mother was an army dependent. In August of 1942, via the Port of Krasnovodsk on the Caspian Sea, we left 'the inhuman soil' forever.

Mother, Irena and I landed at the port of Pahlevi and were reunited in Teheran, Persia. A radio telegram reached us from our father who, after the fall of France, managed to get to Britain and was helping with the defensive work against the expected German invasion from Norway, defending the eastern seaboard of Scotland. When that threat had receded, he joined the 1st Independent Polish Army under British command. We were all reunited and started our civilian life together in Lundin Links. I worked in Glasgow but, after marrying a Scots lassie, I decided to make Leven my new home and brought up my family of three sons and a daughter. My second son, Raymond, is here today.

By way of a note, I would like to add:

As early as 5th December 1939, the fate of Polish Military Settlers was decided by NKVD Commissar for Internal Security of the USSR, Lawrentye Beria, and sealed by Stalin's signatures of 19th and 25th December 1939.

In his note, Beria tells Stalin that we are hardened Polish patriots, participants, wives and children of Polish soldiers who contributed to the Polish victory over the Red Army in 1920. Not being suitable for Soviet Rehabilitation, therefore, he proposed to deport us to Siberian labour camps as Special Deportees. 'Spiecpieriesiedlencow and guests of NKVD'. (Document Nr 2001-558)

Altogether 26,790 families, 139,286 people in all, were deported to Siberia on 10th February 1940. There were three other major deportations to follow. The total number of deportees was approximately 1,200,000 civilians.

A similar document went to Stalin on 5th March 1940, and was approved by him regarding the fate of Polish Officers and Intelligentsia. They were either shot in Katyn, Miednoye, or drowned in the White Sea in April of 1949.

The civilised world knew of the massacres perpetrated by the NKVD, but remained silent about it until 1989 when President Gorbachev admitted to the atrocities. In 1990 Boris Yeltsin handed the NKVD special files to the President of Poland. Special Deportees awaited the same fate, but by different means.

Lech Muszyński on his first meeting since September 1939 with his father. Leven, summer 1945

Michael Zawada
Polish Navy

Glasgow

I was born in August 1921 in a small village near Czestochowa. The village did not see many changes since the Russians annexed it in 1794. In 1922 my parents emigrated from Poland to the Champagne Region of France to work on a farm with horses. This area had been devastated during the First World War. For us children there was a lot of fun from the relics and scars left by the savage campaign where so many gave their lives.

At the outbreak of the Second World War, I was not called up by the French as I was a Polish citizen. In September 1939, I received papers from the Polish Government to present myself for a medical examination and in November 1939, I volunteered for the Polish Navy. I was called up in February 1940.

Our training in France began at Coetquidean and then moved to Pontchâteau in Brittany. Living conditions there were not of the best but it was supposed to be part of our training. Our beds were of straw in an old hayloft above a stable and our washing facilities were a nearby river. Our uniforms and equipment were outdated and from the Napoleonic War era. In mid April, we received our Polish Navy uniforms and made allegiance to serve Poland. On the 23rd April, we left Pontchâteau for Le Havre. Our journey was by train in wagons that were designed for transporting horses. When we arrived at Southampton, we travelled by Third Class coach and we thought we had landed on another planet. We arrived at Plymouth and were welcomed by British and Polish military personnel.

We began training for our speciality on an old converted merchant ship which had been renamed *Gdynia* and was the Polish Navy base – I was trained as a gunner at *HMS Drake*. During my training I injured my knee and have suffered with it until this very day. We were trained on several types of guns, including anti aircraft guns and four and six-inch guns.

We were all greatly disappointed when France collapsed in 1940. The French crews were removed from their ships by the British to prevent them from returning to occupied France. The vessels *Pomerol, Ouragan, Medoc* and a small 'chasseur' were transferred to us. These ships flew the Polish White Eagle and the Tricolour simultaneously as they were French vessels with a Polish Crew. Later, they were manned by British crews but retained the Polish officers and they then flew the White Ensign as well. On the 10th July 1940, I went to serve on the *Pomerol*. She was coal driven and could only do twelve knots. We patrolled the Channel alone, under both Polish and French flags, expecting every day the German invasion of Great Britain. We had one 75mm and a 37mm gun on board. Each patrol was a day or two long and the crew of this ship were entirely Polish.

In September of 1940, the Germans bombed Devonport heavily and my ship was badly damaged below the water line. The water came in and we worked all night pumping out trying to balance the ship. Eventually she had to go into dry dock for repairs. Later I was sent to another ship, the *Ouragan,* which was a French Destroyer with a Polish crew. With us we had a British signalman and five other British crewmen. In December 1940, I remember we went to escort a convoy to Iceland and then we went to Orkney and Shetland as part of the Home Fleet escort for *HMS Hood.* Off the Shetlands, we were caught in a very bad storm. At Scapa Flow, I did not go ashore but I formed a bad impression of the place; there was so little daylight. I thought, 'What a place, you hardly see the sun, it is always raining or snowing and nothing grows.'

Suffering knee problems again, I was then sent to Plymouth in March to the sickbay on the *Gdynia* where we had three nights of bombing, and in April I was in Devonport where we had five nights of intensive bombing and all the ships around us were sunk. Shortly afterwards, I came back to Glasgow and I went to Govan to the Polish Depot and the destroyer *Burza.* We went from the Clyde via Londonderry escorting convoys to Iceland. My ship had been built in France and there were problems with the engines. We complained that when the ship went into the shipyards for repairs, the workers did not work and did not do a good job. In fact our Captain wrote a letter of complaint.

We escorted several convoys from Londonderry and Belfast to Iceland and Canada and also brought back return convoys from these parts. The biggest convoy we escorted was made up of some sixty-seven ships and in this period none were lost. In September, I was again disabled with knee problems and in January 1942, I was sent to the Western General Hospital in Edinburgh. I got better and in March 1942, I joined the Polish ship *Błyskawica* which was a destroyer built in the Isle of Wight in 1937 for the Polish Navy. We were on convoy duties to Iceland from Gourock and Londonderry but she was not very good in Atlantic sea conditions as she had been designed for service in the Baltic.

Between October 1942 and May 1943, I served in the Mediterranean on the *Błyskawica*. We escorted a convoy to Malta during which two Spitfires were lost when they ran out of fuel and we also escorted the aircraft carrier *HMS Formidable*. In the Mediterranean, we were attacked by the Germans all of the time and we patrolled constantly against both the Germans and the Italians. During that time we took part in operation 'Torch', the invasion of North Africa, and suffered in action three dead and forty-four wounded. There were 104 holes in the *Błyskawica* after the action. In May and June 1943, we returned to the Isle of Wight for a refit and then we returned to Scapa, and from there patrolling all the way to Norway, escorting the aircraft carriers *Furious, Formidable* and *Implacable* which were engaged in the bombing of the *Tirpitz*.

In early 1944, we were in Newcastle, Scapa, Rosyth and Invergordon and in May of that year, we were back in Plymouth patrolling for the invasion of Europe. On the 8th June 1944, we were in action against three German destroyers off Ushant. I remember it was one o'clock in the morning but with all of the gunfire and flares, it was like daylight. Two German ships were sunk that night and one British ship was hit.

In November 1944, we again went for a refit and when the war in Europe finished we were in a camp in the Isle of Wight. All of our ships were under refit and we knew that after the Yalta agreement, Poland had been sold out. That summer, we sailed to Oban and Tobermory training to go to the Far East. We asked why we were going as Japan was not our enemy. Then Japan surrendered and the war was finally over.

During the war, we all hoped to return to Poland as heroes but the Yalta agreement meant we could not go back for political reasons. Eventually I came to Glasgow to the Radio and TV College and was demobilised on the 29th July 1947. I then went to agricultural college in Glasgow. I became a builder in 1949 and I had my own business from 1960 until 1982.

Michael Zawada

Part II

Early Writings

Memoirs: September 1939 – May 1948
Wiesław Szczygieł
(Lt. Col. George Harvey)

31st August 1939

First day of general mobilisation. Everywhere the atmosphere is good. Military transports are moving westwards. I go by train to Przemyśl to report to the 4th Engineers' Regiment. The train is full of mobilised men and families evacuated from the north of Poland. Everybody is in good spirits. By noon I arrive in the busy town of Przemyśl.

1st September 1939

The war with Germany has started. The radio reports the state of war and the air attacks on several towns including Warsaw. The German army crosses our borders in several places.

2nd, 3rd, 4th September 1939

Unfortunately the news is not good; more and more towns are bombed. We hear that the railway station in Lwów is destroyed. Germans are advancing all the time. Our railway movement is becoming difficult. We are consoled by every crumb of better news or gossip. Apparently there is a counter-attack being prepared at Rzeszów. Here, in the town, there is a lot of excitement increased by air alarms. So far there have been no bombs in Przemyśl, but I don't know what is happening in my nearby home town, Jarosław. My duties here are negligible; the call-up men are arriving slowly.

5th September 1939

I have little to do here. I ask for a few hours off duty and go to the goods railway station where my father is the manager. I learn that he has been off ill for a few days. As I have no news from home, I try to get to Jarosław; it is only thirty odd kilometres away. I manage to get a lift on a hospital train going west. We reach only Radymno; the train can't go any further – the lines are damaged. We are stuck just a few kilometres from Jarosław. At 5 p.m., a squadron of German planes flies over in the direction of Przemyśl. We hear detonations. Shortly they return, shoot up our train and go over Jarosław. I can see and hear explosions; they are probably bombing the railway station there and our house is not far from it. It will soon be dark. I can't go to Jarosław as I couldn't return to the barracks in Przemyśl before midnight. Luckily, at a level crossing I hitch a lift on a vehicle going to Przemyśl.

6th September 1939

I have been posted as a deputy platoon commander at the Regiment's Reserve Battalion. I start training the called-up reservists, some of them twice my age. The news from the front is that the government has left Warsaw. The constant bombing of towns causes chaos. I have no news from home. In the afternoon there is the second bombing of Przemyśl.

The attack is on the station, but a nearby large building is destroyed with many people killed.

7th September 1939

7th September 1939

The situation is becoming worse. We really don't know where the Germans are. New air raids, new bombardments, new losses among the population. Such is war, such is the 'Blitzkrieg' which we did not believe in – now we are bearing the consequences. The enemy is superior in air force and tanks and is paralysing our mobilisation during these first few days of war.

8th September 1939

From early morning we are on the outskirts of the town preparing anti-tank defences. There is feverish activity preparing the roadblocks under difficult conditions as there is an unending stream of refugees, some in lorries, some on foot, some in horse-drawn carts. These are demoralised people: some are civilians, some soldiers without equipment. We are needing a wagon, so we stop one with two horses. There is a colonel in it, quite devastated; he says his regiment has been decimated. He just managed to escape. We can't believe this; we young can't comprehend it. It may be true; we have not the experience of war at first hand.

9th September 1939

It is Saturday. At dawn we return to the barracks. The HQ offices are all packed for evacuation. The whole town is evacuating; the streets are empty, some buildings are in ruins. The 'Roma' cinema, bombed on Thursday, is still burning. We expect to receive any moment an order to evacuate: Przemyśl will not be defended. The defence is to be organised somewhere near Stanisławów. All this indicates that the situation is very bad – the Germans must be very near. At noon I receive an order to deliver orders to one of the companies preparing the demolition of bridges on the river San in the vicinity of Stare Miasto and Krzeszów. I have no idea where it is but it is in the direction of Jarosław – I may be able to drop into our home there. I have a motorbike with a sidecar and a driver and by 2 p.m. we arrive in Jarosław but first I have to deliver orders at the front line. Jarosław doesn't look damaged but Radymno is ruined; in the fields are lying swollen corpses of horses and cattle shot by the German planes.

The roads are choked with refugees going east with lorries, cars, carts, ambulances and civilians on foot. The small town of Leżajsk is deserted. Everyone is either hiding in their houses or escaping. The few people we meet maintain that the Germans are nearby. The railway station is in ruins, as are two nearby villages. Past Leżajsk, I find the Sappers' Company. They are dismantling the demolition charges on the bridges. I don't know why. I meet some of my colleagues who seem to be more optimistic than I am.

On delivering the orders, I return and arrive in Jarosław at 18.00. Looking for petrol, I stop near my old High School. While waiting for my driver who is searching for petrol, I start a conversation with a lady who maintains that there was a gas attack – another rumour. During the conversation I hear the tragic news: during the bombardment the other day our house was demolished. Several people were killed, the parents are in hospital, Zbyszek saved. The lady says there is no use in going to the house in Lachmanówka.

I rush to the hospital. The gates are closed, so I scale the fence. Inside, the view is tragic; the wounded are lying on stretchers in the corridors, the wards are packed, resounding with the cries of the wounded. I find my mother in one of the beds. She is suffering from burns on the neck but otherwise is not too bad. We both cry with joy that in spite of everything we manage to see each other. I hear that father is seriously wounded as well as several other relatives and a few are dead. I talk for a few more minutes; I try to console my mother who suggests that Zbyszek should go to Stryj where it may be safer. I go to my father. He is very ill and weak. He recognises me and is pleased that I have come to see him. It is getting late. I have to go, saying the last goodbyes. I leave with a heavy heart – my head bursting with thoughts, thoughts …

Zbyszek and Babcia are at the Wiśniowskis. There we come to the conclusion that it will be better for Zbyszek to remain in Jarosław. More goodbyes and I am on my way back to Przemyśl.

It is dusk by now but the road is still full of refugees: cars, trucks, guns, horses and pedestrians. My driver curses the darkness – no full lights allowed but at least we are back in Przemyśl. I report my return and describe the situation at the front. A few hours attempted sleep does not come as my head is full of thoughts and tragic impressions of the last few hours. I don't even know if I've slept when the reveille sounds and parade takes place after a short breakfast. The unit is evacuating; we have deserted Przemyśl with fires still burning. Artillery fire rumbles and flashes in the west and in front of us is the glare of the rising sun, maybe with the promise of a better tomorrow.

10th September 1939

10th September 1939

A full day's march towards the east. We manage to commandeer some carts, horses and bicycles so our progress is easier in spite of the crowded roads.

11th September 1939

By dawn we are in Sambor: everywhere there is the same chaos. Among the ruined houses trails the snake of refugees – east, east: it may be safer there. Suddenly there is the sound of approaching planes. We park the wagons under the roadside trees and shelter in the roadside trenches. Nearer and nearer the sound of planes and soon we see them lowering their flight towards us. We see the flashes of their machine gun fine and hear the sound like hail hitting the ground nearby. Soon they are above us and three black specks drop from one of the planes. A terrifying whistle and explosions penetrate the ears.

The air pressure presses me to the ground and a shower of earth falls. They miss us, but from the other side of the road the sound of casualties rends the air. I cross the road and see the damage caused by the bombs. There are three craters in the field and among them several corpses and wounded soldiers and civilians – three of them from my unit. We render first aid and bury the dead; there is no time for funeral rights, just a short prayer for the casualties of war beyond the front line. We leave the site of carnage.

At midday, a short rest and then we carry on. We approach Drochobycz. In the distance we see the glare of burning oil tanks. The horizon seems to be on fire. We enter the town, passing the ruined and burning buildings. Karpaty and Galicja refineries are ablaze.

12th September 1939

At noon we approach Stryj, my birthplace, and stop at the outskirts. I meet people who remember my grandfather and father. Suddenly, there is an air raid warning. The noise of planes and the familiar sight of explosive flashes, sounds and colours of smoke rising from the station buildings and the train which stopped there. The planes disappear and our ineffective machine-gun fire stops. It turns out that a food transport train has been bombed. The population help themselves to sides of bacon, bread, tins of food and barrels of beer. Our soldiers take the chance of supplementing our food supplies and bring two sides of bacon, small barrels of beer and army biscuits.

As our departure from Stryj is scheduled for the evening, I visit aunt and uncle Langner and share my tragic family news with them. At nightfall we depart from Stryj, passing the ruins of buildings and I leave the town of my birth and early childhood with a heavy heart. Will I ever see this town again?

13th, 14th, 15th, 16th, September 1939

We continue our march through Muszyna, Dolina and

Katuszyn and finally to Halicz where from early morning we start preparing defences in the direction of Lwów, which, according to rumours, is being attacked by the Germans. There is news of heavy fighting round Modlin, Warsaw and Kutno.

17th September 1939

All day we work on the outskirts of Halicz, preparing anti-tank defences with the help of the civilian population. We prepare the demolition of the crossing of the river Dniestr. It is Sunday, the sun is shining and it helps to give us a touch of optimism in spite of the distant sound of planes. In the evening, we observe the distant flashes of artillery fire from the direction of Lwów. Our optimistic dreams of an improvement of the situation are broken by the least expected news: the Bolshevik Red Army has crossed our borders and is progressing into the country. We abandon the defences and depart in the direction of Stanisławow.

18th September 1939

Monday. We arrive in Stanisławow in the morning. The town is busy but there is no panic. According to rumours, the Red Army has entered Tarnopol and Kołomyja. Apparently they treat the population correctly and do not interfere with our troops. There are other rumours that the Red Army is going to help us against the Germans.

At nine, the town president appeals to the population to keep calm and to take a friendly attitude to the Red Army which is expected to arrive in hours. We leave the town in the direction of Nadwórna. On the road there is the usual traffic of evacuees in cars, lorries and carts. We arrive in Nadwórna in the evening. It is obvious now that we are evacuating to Hungary but nobody knows any details. We carry on. On hearing the news that we are to cross the Hungarian border, some of the soldiers leave our convoy to return to their homes. Others, especially regular army people, decide to stay and fight if possible. Nobody really knows what to do. We stop in Jaremcze station. I recall my last holiday there in a Scout camp a few years ago.

21ˢᵗ September 1939

Thursday. We are in Jabłonica where we cross the Hungarian frontier still with our arms, but a few kilometres further on, we are obliged to deposit them. And so we finish our 'glorious' campaign. In three weeks the army has disintegrated. We are being interned: officers and cadets are separated from other ranks and transported by train past Budapest and Lake Balaton to the south of Hungary.

25ᵗʰ September 1939

We arrive in Lengeltoty, south of Lake Balaton and are accommodated in a large and elegant but quite empty country house in a large park.

26ᵗʰ September 1939

We have settled down in fairly primitive conditions, sleeping on straw mattresses under army blankets. The food is reasonable and we get two Pengos a day for personal expenses. We are allowed to visit the nearby small town and surrounding area where the local population is very friendly and full of sympathy for us.

And what is happening in the rest of the world? Well, England and France are at war with Germany but the activities are limited to some artillery exchanges, air reconnaissance and a naval blockade of Germany.

I write letters to Poland. Maybe we can manage to make contact. I also write twice to Uncle Namysłowski who is Polish Consul General in Budapest. The future is bleak; the only solution would be to get to France where the Polish army is forming. The days are passing monotonously with the last blinks of summer but they do not brighten my dull mood.

2nd October 1939

2nd October 1939

Three of my co-internees have escaped, probably to France. Others are also talking about it and preparing.

15th October 1939

A letter from uncle Włodek arrives with an invitation for me to come to Budapest. Maybe it will be easier to go to France from there.

16th October 1939

There comes confidential news that there will be a semi-official departure of volunteers to France. We are preparing for this by having our passport photographs taken at the local photographer's.

18th October 1939

In spite of the preparations, I decide to go to uncle in

Budapest. I sell my officer's boots and the rest of the uniform, including my lovely greatcoat, to the older officers who do not intend to go to France, and with the meagre Pengos received, I buy the cheapest possible civilian suit in the local shop as I can't travel in my uniform.

19th October 1939
In the afternoon, as a civilian, I walk out of the camp, go to the railway station, and by the evening I arrive in Budapest – no problems. Budapest is quite impressive – reminds me of Warsaw, which, by now, is in ruins. I am received very cordially in uncle's nice home. His German wife, quite a pleasant, large blond, and two boys, Janusz and Jerzyk (five and seven years approximately) greet me and they feed me there. I relate my war experiences until late into the night.

20th October 1939 onwards
I am settled in Uncle's home at 11 Stephany Utca, have my own bedroom, play with the boys and explore Budapest, a lovely city. The matter of going to France isn't so simple. Uncle has not been working since his heart attack and his office is run, according to him, by the Polish Intelligence Service, although he is still unofficially in contact with the Polish Minister. He thinks my duty is to consider my family in Poland especially as the situation in France and England is not all that good. The phoney war is still going on. Germany has incorporated Silesia, Pomorze and the Poznań area into the German State. The Soviets have incorporated the territories east of San and Bug; the rest of Poland is under

German occupation. Apparently there is still partisan fighting going on in Poland.

10th November 1939

First news from mother, in a post card in German, about father's death. This is terrible news. I cannot even comment on this. His funeral was on the 13th September.

11th November 1939

Another letter from mother and Wiśniewskis where mother and Zbyszek are staying. Zbyszek is starting some school. Włodek C is wounded in Tarnopol. There were ten people killed during the bombing of our house. This took place on 5th September.

22nd November 1939

I am still at Uncle's, waiting, I don't know what for. The war is stagnant, limited to small air raids and naval attacks on British merchant ships. The Germans are boasting every day about more sinking, using magnetic mines. Today I meet some men from the internment camp – they are going to France today and are surprised that I haven't yet left. More letters from mother and Zbyszek – no special news. They are clearing the ruins of the house. In the papers (German) there is news of the sinking of the *MS Piłsudski* by a mine.

27th November 1939

A new war is developing in Europe. There have been frontier skirmishes between Finland and the Soviets.

30th November 1939

The expected conflict in Finland has developed into a full-scale Soviet attack on land, sea and air. Several Finnish towns bombed – the navy active in the Baltic.

2nd December 1939

The Soviets are occupying more of the Finnish territories. The Finnish Government resigns. Roosevelt's appeal for peace is rejected by Molotov (USSR Foreign Minister).

25th December 1939

A QUIET, sad Christmas with the Namysłowski family. Uncle buys me a decent suit and coat as winter begins to bite.

January, February, March 1940

Nothing new is happening. The war in the west is stagnant. The Soviets and Finns are still fighting. Uncle got a job in the Yugoslavian Ministry of Finance and has departed there, followed by his family. He wanted me to go with the rest of the family. I have decided to go to France via the transport organised by the Polish Office at the Consulate.

2nd April 1940

By train from Budapest to the Hungarian/Yugoslav frontier at Baboczy which we cross 'secretly' and illegally at night. At dawn we are received by the Yugoslav border police and transported to Zagreb where we stay for a few days awaiting arrangements to go by train to France via Italy which, luckily, is not yet at war with the Allies.

6th April 1940

An interesting journey with a group of officers by comfortable train through the north of Italy, via Milan and Turin.

7th April 1940

Arrived at Modane in France and transported to a transit camp – back to primitive conditions. We spend two weeks in a camp near Tours where we are issued with French uniforms but no arms. Apparently there is a shortage of rifles in France. We get acquainted with French cuisine which bears no resemblance to the French cuisine we have read about. The menus are only brightened by a quarter of a litre of *vin ordinaire* with every main meal.

I am still a sergeant officer cadet and according to French regulations, the pay is meagre – enough for a packet of 'Troop' cigarettes a week. Luckily I don't smoke. My verification to 2nd Lieutenant is bogged down somewhere in the Polish Government offices in Paris. Don't know how long it will take to come through.

15th April 1940

Have been posted to the 3rd Engineers' Battalion which is stationed in a small town on the Loire, near Angers.

Here conditions aren't all that good. A few of us cadets of various ranks and mainly reserve, not regular army, are billeted in an attic of a farmhouse. Conditions are very primitive – so is the food. Polish cooks using French provisions!

The organisation and training of the engineers, mainly reservists of Polish origin who settled in France, progress slowly. There is a lack of equipment; even rifles are ex-First World War. The French population is anti-war and anti-army. As an example: on a route march exercise we stop at a farm and ask for a glass of water for which we are charged five *centimes* each.

May – 1st June 1940

But it is summer weather – the river Loire is nearby, so an occasional swim refreshes us but doesn't kill the lice in our clothes which haven't been washed in hot water for weeks.

Unfortunately the war news is not good. The German army invaded Holland and Belgium, bypassed the famous French Maginot Line and entered France without much resistance. The British Expeditionary Force is withdrawing and eventually evacuating at Dunkirk under constant German attacks.

17th June 1940

France surrenders – Germans are in Paris. Our army is in disarray: 1st Division decimated; 2nd Division evacuated to Switzerland; our third and other units evacuate to the West of France to the ports in the hope of sea evacuation to England which is determined to fight. There is general panic. Roads are choked with refugees and French soldiers who abandon their arms, only keep their *bidons* – one litre water bottles filled with wine.

Our Engineers' Battalion commandeers a goods train and we evacuate westwards. The French railway authorities let us pass after being threatened. The train engine is driven by our own crew with a machine-gun at the front. There are no ships at the nearest ports so our train heads south to Bordeaux where we are told to head further south as the Bordeaux harbour is bombed. The following night we arrive in St Jean de Luz (almost on the border with Spain). Luckily, here is the Polish liner *MS Sobieski* anchored outside the harbour. We and hundreds of other Polish and some French evacuees are ferried by tender to the liner – what a happy coincidence – a Polish ship to save us from either capture by the Germans or internment in a hostile Spain. By dawn we depart into the unknown. The ship is overloaded; as well as accommodation for 1200 passengers there are 4000 military and civilian evacuees who are accommodated in cabins, lounges, corridors and decks. At breakfast, there are queues for both dining rooms. The food is good and plentiful, served by a friendly Polish crew. By lunchtime, after a few hours of sailing in the Bay of Biscay, the queues are much smaller and by evening meal time, there are no queues at all – *mal de mer* has solved the problem.

During the two days' and nights' journey which seemed unnecessarily long to reach England, we had several alarms when everybody had to assemble at life-boat stations with life-jackets. Needless to say, there were not enough lifejackets or enough room for everybody in the lifeboats. We were told that these were drill alerts – just in case!

22nd June 1940
A lovely morning and the lack of ship's movement wakens us to see the green landscape surrounding a large port town.

While we wait for disembarkation, I call on one of the ship's officers whom I knew from our internment time in Hungary. Before we say our last farewells with a glass of *Wyborowa,* he tells me that we have arrived off Plymouth and explains that our long journey took us out into the mid-Atlantic to avoid the lurking German U-boats. Our 'drill' alarms were real.

We disembark from tenders which deposit us in the harbour where we are greeted by pleasant English ladies in various uniforms. They offer us cups of tea (with milk and sugar), cakes, cigarettes and more smiles. What a difference from our previous French hosts. We board the trains – and have another surprise: no more goods wagons, but passenger carriages with soft seats for six men in a compartment. Without much delay, the train sets off into the green countryside, passing tidy villages and towns. At dusk we disembark and are marched off to a tented, huge camp spread out on a racecourse. We don't know where we are as all the names of stations were removed as one of the anti-invasion precautions. Our knowledge of English geography and language is negligible and all the stations we passed were called either CRAVEN 'A', GOLD FLAKE or BOVRIL.

The camp is somewhat chaotic; there are thousands of various troops milling about, but we are adequately fed and bedded. Some of us venture out to the town neighbouring the camp. The inhabitants are friendly and smiling, offering us cups of tea and cakes – not many signs of war here. We are impressed by the tidy streets and solid housing.

After a few days in the camp, the various units are sorted out and we board another train. We seem to be heading north. The scenery changes from flat to hilly and eventually mountainous, but the mountains are somehow gentle and bare – hardly any trees. The weather also changes from warm and sunny to less so. After many hours of travel, we pass a large industrial township stretching for miles and by dusk we stop at a small station among hills and mountains. The news spreads: this is Scotland, our final destination – a bit of a 'let-down'. The camp is nearly ready. The tents are a peculiar conical shape, the field wet. Back to field kitchen, cold water and open-air latrines. But we are sappers, and soon everything will be organised.

Scotland doesn't seem to be so bad. This is mid-summer, the weather not continental but there are many nice days with a few showers. The days are long; it does not get dark until after 10 p.m. The life in the camp settles into a routine of improving the camp, some exercises and of course occasional sessions of drill – just to occupy the troops. The nearby small township, Crawford, doesn't provide much entertainment. There is only one pub, and the few girls are locked up at dusk. Those of us, myself among them, who are keen to learn the strange language, attend daily lessons conducted by one of our officers who apparently knows the language. There are no books to help us, but somebody acquires a Polish/English handbook designed for Poles in America. This is divided, chapter by chapter, and circulated daily amongst those keen to learn. I learn by heart at least a page a day.

August 1940

Since our engineers' company is more or less intact, we are posted to Johnstone, a town near Paisley and Glasgow. This is better. The men are accommodated in the town hall. It is dry, the food passable and what is more important, we are doing concrete sappers' work. We are bussed daily to a Rolls Royce factory to build defences, repair bomb damage, pillboxes and even have the task of digging up unexploded bombs which were dropped by a sneak German raider. Evenings and Sundays are free, so there is a chance to go to the town and spend the pay which is much better than the meagre French francs.

We begin to learn the language by being in contact with the local population which is very friendly. So are the girls!

The language is still a problem. There are no Polish-English dictionaries. I acquire a pocket English-German dictionary which helps a lot. It doesn't tell us about local customs and that there are no bars open on a Sunday. Another officer cadet and I take a bus to Paisley. There is a café open, which, according to our French experience, should have wine and beer available. We ask for beer. No beer, but there is ginger beer. We buy a bottle each, pour out the foaming white liquid and taste. The taste is a horrible, soapy-tasting lemonade. It puts me off ginger beer for life.

The next big adventure is a weekend with my pal in Glasgow. On arrival by bus one Saturday afternoon, we go in search of some night time accommodation. A hotel is financially impossible but according to the camp grapevine, bed & breakfast establishments are good and reasonably priced. After walking up and down Bath Street we choose one and book in with the help of sign language and my German dictionary. The price is five shillings a head, including a bath and breakfast.

The bath is the greatest luxury: my first hot bath since leaving Budapest in April. The other luxury is what is now called 'the full Scottish breakfast'. We cannot believe the spread and this is at the end of the first year of the war. There is porridge, cereals, grapefruit, toast, marmalade, bacon, sausages and eggs. We don't know where to start. We repeat our weekend trips to Glasgow once or twice before our company is posted to Lossiemouth in North-East Scotland to build coastal defences there.

• •

September 1940

No sooner had our company arrived at Lossiemouth than I, along with two officers and two sergeants, was sent to an English Engineers' Company in Yorkshire, near Scarborough, to acquaint ourselves with the British Army engineers' equipment and way of working. We were posted to different platoons which were building coastal defences there. Our Polish countrymen met up only once or twice for a demonstration and as I was the most advanced in English, I had the task of interpreting for my compatriots. The two weeks spent on my own among the Yorkshiremen had been my best training in English: I just had to speak and try to understand some of the broad Yorkshire accent.

This was the beginning of September, the start of the Battle of Britain and the threat of the German invasion.

One night, there was a general alert because of some news of an invasion. I was at that time with the Company HQ in Bridlington. We manned our allocated defence positions. I was still wearing my French uniform and helmet. I was promptly issued with the British 'tin hat' and gas mask as the Company CO had said, 'He will be the first to be shot with that strange helmet on.'

Luckily it was a false alarm. We were stood down by dawn and shortly afterwards our Polish groups returned to our Company in Lossiemouth.

17th September 1940

My birthday and good news: the verification of my commission as 2nd Lieutenant has at last come through. With it, the first star on my shoulders, and officer's pay and even quite a handsome sum of back pay. Our posting in Lossiemouth soon ended with the Company transfer to Fife.

The train took us to Leuchars from where we marched the few miles to Tentsmuir Forest, where we had to erect the tents as our quarters. Our company's task was to build a permanent Nissan-hut camp for a battalion which was to defend this part of Fife. As a newly-fledged 2nd Lieutenant, I didn't have an establishment in the Company, so I became an unofficial adjutant of Company Commander, Captain Wajdowicz, who took me under his wing and I shared a tent with him. Soon the Scottish weather set in. The rains of late September and October did not help the troops in their task of building the camp. Many a day it was too wet to work and we spent the hours in the dripping tents chatting and smoking. As the cigarettes came with the rations and there was no French wine or Scottish whisky to barter them for, I started smoking. After all, I was twenty-one. The monotony of the autumn days and evenings was brightened when on Saturdays, the company officers, led by Captain Wajdowicz, went by the company truck to St Andrews. There, in the Tudor café, we had high tea. By that time, the food rationing had begun to bite and you were allowed only one egg, one rasher of bacon and one sausage for your high tea. So we usually had our first high tea, by which time the bar in the adjoining Imperial Hotel was open. After suitable refreshment there, we were back at the Tudor café for our second high tea. Once or twice I went by train to Dundee, where I got my first dress uniform, a Retinette I camera, a leather suitcase and, as an investment, a gold signet ring.

October 1940

The building of the camp progressed and soon the troops arrived. As it happened, it was the 2nd Battalion of the 1st Polish Rifle Brigade that was posted to the camp built by Polish Engineers. One rainy day, there was a commotion in the camp. I ran out with my newly acquired camera and took a few shots of the Battalion being inspected by a group of Polish and British high-ranking officers led by a portly gentleman in a raincoat and a peculiar black hat. It was not until later when my film was developed and printed that I discovered that it was Mr Churchill himself inspecting the 'brave newly-arrived defenders of the UK'.

27th October 1940

I have been posted to the 4th Cadre Canadian Rifle Brigade in Leven. On a rainy October day I arrived by truck in Leven. The weather did not improve my first impression which was 'what a dump' after the autumn charms of Tentsmuir Forest and the elegance of ancient St Andrews. I did not imagine that I would spend most of my life in Leven.

It turned out that the Brigade was really a Cadre, consisting of a few hundred officers stationed in Leven, Lundin Links, Largo and Elie. My first posting was to the only unit consisting of other ranks. This was the Brigade's administration platoon, billeted in the local Masonic Hall. The platoon consisted of an assortment of cooks, clerks and other odd-bods obviously decanted from other units and not first-line soldiers. It was commanded by a middle-aged captain (I don't remember his name). I was to be his second-in-command but the unit was ruled by a formidable old-fashioned sergeant major.

Luckily, my posting there did not last too long and I was transferred to an engineers' HQ department called Unit 124 which was accommodated in a small room at the top floor of the Brigade's HQ in the YWCA building in Church Road. The unit consisted of Lt Col Balcerowicz, Major Moździerz, Captain Kordel, Lts Benon Zawadzki, Victor Zub-Zdanowicz and myself. Our task was planning the defences of Fife.

This was a rather theoretical task consisting of paper work based on terrain reconnaissance and maps. During my first weeks in Leven, I was billeted with a delightful old couple, Mr and Mrs Brown in East Links overlooking the golf course and the sea, with its picturesque autumn sunrises when I walked from my billet to the officers' mess in the Birchlee for breakfast at the west end of the town.

The local population was very friendly and we were asked to their homes for evening entertainment. In one of these houses, that of Mr and Mrs Andrew, there was a party one night where I met my future wife Kathleen – a beautiful redhead.

December 1940
Our unit, No 124, consisting by then of a few more officers, viz Captain Grocholski, Lts Patkowski and Micis, was transferred to Elie and Earlsferry where we were billeted and fed in the Palmira boarding house. We spent a rather dull and depressing Christmas there. The winter months were cold and wet with not much to do. The evenings were spent in studying English and playing bridge, lubricated by an occasional bottle of whisky.

January – End of Spring 1941
In great secrecy, some of us were sent on a 'cloak-and-dagger' course in Inverlochy Castle near Fort William. Here we were back to the Nissan Huts and washing in the freezing stream nearby (it was too far to the toilet block). At least the programme was interesting – training in 'reflex' shooting, use of explosives and booby traps, night exercises and climbing Ben Nevis. We were all sworn to secrecy as this was, as we later discovered, the preliminary training and selection for being sent for underground work in occupied Poland. Not all were selected for further secret training but

this was the beginning of the formation of our future Parachute Brigade. The spring saw the creation of the 'Monkey Grove' or 'Małpi Gaj' in Largo House.

The engineer officers and one or two other ranks with technical skills started constructing parachute training contraptions among the old outbuildings and trees of the grounds of Largo House.

May – June 1941

After two weeks' preliminary para training on the contraptions of the Monkey Grove, which I myself participated in constructing, I was sent with a group of other 'volunteers' with some of our instructors for real para training to Ringway Airport near Manchester where there was an RAF para training school. After some more physical training and instructions, we donned the parachutes, embarked with trepidation the Whitely plane, sat at the hole in the floor of the plane and when the green light came, and the instructor shouted 'GO!' you just swung your legs into the hole, closed your eyes and jumped. When the chute opened, your eyes opened too to see a white cross on the ground – a bad omen? No, the landing was not painful and the same procedure was repeated several times during the following days at Ringway, but I must confess that the apprehension of jumping did not diminish with practice. After the two weeks' training, we were considered qualified parachutists and were awarded the badge of the diving eagle and three shillings a day pay enhancement.

Summer 1941

The organisation and training of the future Para Brigade continued to progress. Our 'Sosab' (Sosabowski) was full of ideas: one of these was the establishment of a camp near Dunkeld for the purpose of training officers and officer cadets in field-craft and watercraft. As a sapper, I was posted there as a watercraft instructor on the river Tay. Back to the life in tents and the rigours of the Scottish weather! On the whole, I enjoyed the three months of rough living in one of the prettiest parts of Scotland. There was shooting, fishing, boating, river fording, mountain climbing, campfire cooking and when the skies opened, plenty of bridge in the tents. At that time I still had my second-hand motorbike which I had bought the previous year for £15. This allowed me to visit other nearby parts of Scotland and make an occasional weekend trip to Leven to meet Kathleen.

September 1941

By this time, the 4th Cadre Rifle Brigade has been reinforced by volunteers from other Polish units which were being reorganised in Scotland and there were over 300 para-trained officers and men among us. Our Sosab organised a show to impress our Polish and British authorities. Using the 'Whitleys' from Ringway, an exercise to simulate an attack on the heavy artillery battery on Kincraig was performed. It was a historic day, not only for the Polish Army but also for Scotland when a company of paratroopers descended from the skies over the shooting range and fields of Shell Bay. It was a historic moment for the Brigade as, at the end of the successful exercise, General Sikorski, Polish Prime Minister, in his speech announced that 'From today, you are the 1st Polish Independent Parachute Brigade.' I personally was not required to jump that day, but, as a sapper, I took part in simulating the battle effects by exploding charges among the 'attacking' troops.

From now on, the tempo of training and activities in the Brigade increased. All officers were being sent on all sorts of courses. In the winter there was the skiing course in Huntly. When my turn came there was hardly any snow left and our training consisted of exploring the local hills with the skis on our shoulders. Later, with some other sapper officers, I was sent to the British Engineers' Centre in Elgin to acquaint ourselves with the RE equipment. We were billeted in the Grand Hotel where a good time was had by all. An incident in my 'war' adventures worth mentioning was my trip to London to bring half a ton of explosives by passenger train – but that's another story.

1942

Our Brigade at last received reinforcement: volunteers from the Polish Army in the Middle East, evacuated there from the USSR, now started to arrive for training. The sappers' company was formed under the command of Captain Piotr Budziszewski who arrived from internment in Spain. I was promoted to full lieutenant and given the command of the third platoon. The company was stationed in Elie and accommodated in the Linwood Hotel with the officers billeted in various private houses. My landlady was Mrs Brown, a charming old lady who spoiled her lodger. During our stay in Fife, the engineers' company was posted in Elie,

Pittenweem, Cellardyke and finally in Falkland. My acquaintance with Falkland started earlier when I was posted to the Officer Cadets' School as an engineer instructor. The six months in Falkland were easy, especially as I didn't need to do any hard physical exercises, having been medically released because of some damage to my back.

1943

Back in the company with my platoon. More intensive training on attachment to the Third Battalion posted in Falkland and Freuchie. My platoon was accommodated in Freuchie. I was billeted with a Mrs Fox, another charming old lady who insisted on giving me breakfast in the morning and cocoa at night.

The war situation was beginning to improve for the Allies. The Americans were with us; the German successes in Russia were bogged down. Our training progressed and became more intensive. In Poland the underground Army was fighting, supported by some of the officers trained in our Monkey Grove. This gave our propaganda men in London the idea of producing a film depicting some of our officers' para and underground training here, action in Poland, and a return via Norway to Scotland to be reunited with their Scottish sweethearts. So, one day a Polish Army film unit arrived in Leven to choose the prospective actors. I was one of the 'victims' chosen to undergo a screen test in London.

Mietek Krajewski and I were sent to Pinewood Studios for a few days to undergo quite an exciting experience of being filmed in simulated action. Unfortunately, due to the change in the political situation (the tragic death of General Sikorski among others) the project was dropped and so ended my film career. Back to the company and the daily routine. The company was now stationed in Falkland where we were undergoing intensive training. This didn't pass without accidents, as one of my sappers was killed by an accidental explosion of a charge he was preparing. Luckily I was away somewhere during this exercise which was conducted by my deputy, 2nd Lt Modelski. The tragedy cast a gloom on the whole company, fortunately without disciplinary consequences.

I was then billeted in Falkland with a Mrs Russell, the widow of a police inspector. There were two daughters: one young and good-looking, the other middle-aged, not so pretty, but a hospital sister. They were very kind to me, so that when I complained about my varicose veins, the nurse offered to give me an injection and came from the hospital with the injection, did the necessary preparation, injected my leg and I ... passed out – the first and only time in my life. I kept my varicose veins to have them operated on ten years later.

1944

Our Brigade was almost full strength, and continued intensive training. Our authorities, including Sosab, were planning to use the Brigade in the liberation of Poland, as Germany was under pressure in the war with the USSR in the East and the bombing by the Allies from the West. There was increasing preparation for the 'Second Front', i.e. invasion of the continent from the UK. The British authorities were planning to use our Brigade in this invasion.

6th June 1944

The 'Second Front' had started: British, American and Canadian Forces landed in France. Our Brigade was put under the command of Marshall Montgomery, but not for initial use in the invasion.

3rd July 1944

The Brigade was transferred to East England near Peterborough for final combat training and para drops. The departure from Leven and other Fife towns was emotional. The railway stations were full of the local population saying 'farewell' and 'good luck' to their allies whom they had hosted during the past few years.

Our new accommodation was in tent camps. My company was in a camp near a charming village of Wansford; the training was intensive, route marches day and night with full kit and day and night para drops and manoeuvres. As I had had no conversion exercises to jump from the door of the Dakota - C47 planes, which were our new transport, I volunteered to jump on one of the company exercises just for the experience.

It was a lovely warm July afternoon and after a short flight, we were dropped over an airfield. The rising, still, warm summer air made my jump a pleasant experience. I was converted to jumping from the Dakota. Not so was my next jump on a stormy night when, after two hours of a bumpy flight, almost everybody in my platoon were using the paper bags supplied for the purpose. I was not sick in the plane, but made up for it after landing head first – luckily in a potato field. Other exercises followed, one of them with tragic results when two Dakotas collided in mid-air, killing twenty odd of our paratroopers and both American crews of the planes.

It was lovely summer weather. My Kathleen was on school holidays, so she managed to come for a week and get B & B accommodation in the village. This brightened up my routine and we spent every moment of my free time together. In the meantime, the campaign on the continent was progressing favourably. Not so in Poland as the Warsaw Rising was not progressing well. Not that our desired drop there would have made much difference. As it was, the Dakota's range was not sufficient for a return trip and the Soviets did not agree to their landing and refuelling on their occupied territory.

So we were destined to fight on the Western Front. By the end of July we were considered equipped and ready for action. The first action alert was for Rambouillet, south-east of Paris. Due to the faster advances of the Allied land forces, air landing was not necessary, and this operation was cancelled. The next planned action was for Tournais in Belgium. This also was cancelled and another for Maastricht in Holland was planned and prepared for. This too was cancelled as were the next few operations code-named 'Fifteen' and 'Comet' in Holland.

It was not until mid-September that operation 'Market Garden' took us to Arnhem in Holland. All the aborted operations were very strenuous, both physically and mentally for all ranks as each time we had to plan everything in detail to be ready to take off at a few hours' notice. All troops were briefed, issued with parachutes and even local 'occupation' money.

• •

17th September 1944
The start of the operation 'Market Garden'. It is peculiar that many important events in my life happen near that date: my birthday, the Soviets entering Poland, the verification of my commission, the start of the operation of Arnhem.

The first British units of the 1st Para Brigade land on Dutch soil. Our Brigade is to follow two days later due to lack of sufficient numbers of planes. In the event, we do not drop until the 21st September due to adverse weather conditions. An uneventful flight of a few hours, endangered only by Ack-Ack fire when we reach the continent which is still in German hands. By late sunny afternoon, our planes lower their flight to some 800 feet; we can see clearly the Dutch fields criss-crossed by canals and ditches. 'Five minutes to action stations!' shouts the American crewman. Our 'stick' (my platoon) gets up, we check our chutes and hook up the static lines on the cable running the length of the Dakota.

This is the longest five minutes of the whole flight – standing at the open door of the plane with one eye on exploding black puffs of Ack-Ack shells, with the other on the red light of 'Action Station' in nervous anticipation of the green light for 'GO'. And 'GO it is. You step out into space, feel the rush of air, the jerk of the opening chute. Not much time to admire the flat scenery: enough to see the strings of tracer bullets from a machine-gun on the railway embankment and another Dakota trailing a smoke trail in her mortal dive. The brave American pilots – no chance of them using their chutes. Suddenly the ground rushes towards you; you release the kitbag attached by a long rope. It hits the ground and you follow, collapse the canopy of the chute and try to pull the kitbag to you. It's stuck on a bush and as you rise to get to it, the machine-gun from the railway embankment opens up. Luckily, there is a ditch by which I can get to my kitbag, unload it, and knee-deep in water, proceed by the ditch to the company rendezvous. The rest is another story written, discussed, analysed and filmed: the story of *A Bridge Too Far*. (See page 145)

October 1944
The Brigade returns to England. I go by plane with an advance party to get the camp ready. The bulk of the Brigade follows a few days later by sea transport. We are back in Wansford Camp. I get a captaincy and I am awarded the Krzyż Walecznych (Cross of Valour) for my efforts in organising the crossing of the Rhine. There follows leave for everybody but I am posted to a preliminary course for the Staff School. The course is in Kinghorn so my visits to Leven are frequent.

November 1944 – January 1945
Still physically in Kinghorn most of the time but mentally in a dilemma about the future. The war looks like ending soon but our return to Poland is doubtful. The Soviets are in Poland, the Germans are in retreat. I decide that whatever

happens, my future is with my Kasia. Hence the proposal, enthusiastic acceptance, reluctant approval by parents and an engagement party. I am due a week's leave in February before being posted to Staff School in Peebles, so we decide on a wedding day on the 10th February. As Peter Budziszewski (minus two fingers of his right hand lost at Arnhem) is back with his company in Fife, I ask him to be my 'best man'. He arranges for one of our chaplains, Fr Bednarz, to perform the ceremony in the Chapel at Falkland Palace as I had been stationed previously in Falkland.

10th February 1945

A cold winter's day, snow on the ground, the chapel not heated (it is still war-time). All guests assembled, the nervous groom and his best man waiting in the sacristy but no padré. Frantic phone calls to Cupar. The padré mistook the date – no transport to bring him to Falkland.

Urgent visit to the local priest, Fr Lion, who is reluctant to perform the ceremony as he has no dispensation to perform a 'mixed' service. Some 'arm twisting' with a donation to the Church overcomes the difficulties and after a delay of almost an hour, we are married in a simple and even austere ceremony (no music because of mixed marriage). The freezing cold does not chill our warm hearts and happiness. Outside the chapel a surprise: a guard of honour provided by the sappers of my old platoon. On to lunch in the Lomond Hotel in Freuchie. Photographs at Caithness Bros in Kirkcaldy and train to honeymoon in the Caledonian Hotel in Aberdeen. Our honeymoon is spent in bed as

Kathleen gets a chill and sore throat in the cold chapel. A good excuse!

February – June 1945
Continuation of the Staff School in Black Barony House in Eddleston near Peebles. We are all billeted in private houses in Peebles and bussed daily to the school which has an interesting university-type atmosphere and programme. Most of the lecturers are distinguished staff colonels from the pre-war Staff School in Warsaw. The work is quite hard, the hours long. Too difficult to travel to Leven at weekends but Kathleen comes for some weekends and Easter school holidays. She is now a fully-fledged teacher in Buckhaven Primary.

July 1945
Graduation ceremony in the Staff School, a week's leave and posting to the staff of the HQ of the 1st Corps in Falkirk. The war in Europe is finished (May 1945) but still goes on in the Far East. My Brigade (to which I am not likely to return) is on occupation of Germany, but East Poland is under Soviet occupation and the rest enlarged in the West by some of the former German territories.

The news from Poland is not good. The Communist regime there is not favourable to Polish regular army officers from the West. So, nobody knows what the future will bring. My decision is to remain in Great Britain in the meantime and to think of some occupation for the future. Photography, my hobby, and because of some experience over the last few years, seems to be a possibility. I am in the intelligence department of the HQ and there is a darkroom and a good Leica camera. Another staff officer, Captain Adam Zielinski,[1] and I do some practical work. Another photo opportunity turns up when a photographic course is offered in Glasgow in a former 'cloak and dagger' establishment. This is for me a good few weeks of training by professional photographers.

Autumn – Winter 1945 – 1946
Contact with Poland is limited; we begin to receive letters and to send parcels, mainly with medicines, coffee and clothing. The situation there is still chaotic and conditions very difficult.

　　　Here we are in comparative comfort, but unable to help our family. A Communist government established in Poland is initially recognised by the British Government and the Polish Government in London but has the recognition withdrawn. Our army is being reorganised into the Polish Resettlement Corps. Our Corps HQ is also reorganised. I am posted to a 'Demob' department which keeps me very busy. A great dilemma for all: to return to Poland, to emigrate to Canada or the USA or wherever, or to stay in the UK looking for a job.

　　　We are now nominally in the British Army. The officers have been given the King's commission of Second Lieutenant but 'local' rank equal to their Polish rank. The pay is a little better because we are being paid at British rates.

---

[1] Captain Zielinski later became a medical photographer in the Bridge of Earn Hospital

Spring, Summer, Autumn 1946

The PRC (Polish Resettlement Corps) is in full swing. I am in the 'demob' department, dealing with those who are emigrating or moving to civilian life. Scottish Trade Unions are not eager to admit Poles into anything but labouring jobs. All the better jobs go to the British soldiers being demobbed. Most of our men and even officers go to the coalmines or building sites. At the same time, there are trade training courses in other occupations like tailoring, boot repairing, joinery. All those who can, apply for immigration to the USA, Canada or South America. Others opt to return to Poland. This is being encouraged by the British Authorities and the Warsaw Government but unofficially discouraged by ours here. The majority of officers are reluctant to return and many men originating from East Poland, now incorporated into the USSR, have nowhere to return to.

Winter, Spring 1947

Our corps HQ has been transferred to Polkemet Camp near Whitburn in West Lothian. Back to Nissen Huts and camp life, although quite comfortable. I have a room to myself in a wooden barrack. My duties are not strenuous but interesting as I am a liaison officer from General Maczek to the Scottish Command in Edinburgh. Hence frequent trips there.

Because of this, my first contact with British officialdom, I realise that my surname of Szczygieł might be a hindrance in civilian life. The British officers are finding it difficult to pronounce and spell SZCZ etc, so they ask me for an English approximation. I offer one and from then on I am

Captain Shigel, which amuses General Maczek. 'Who is this Captain Shigel?'

I also stand in as an unofficial adjutant for General Dworak (a very pleasant person). An amusing incident connected with this is when General Dworak (a small rotund man) orders me (a tall slim young officer) to accompany him to the sad ceremony of decommissioning one of the Polish destroyers: *ORP Kujawjak* (or was it Krakowiak?) at the naval base in Rosyth. After the reception in the ship's wardroom and a few pink gins, there is the lowering of the Polish flag and the hoisting of the White Ensign. Leaving the ship after a few more pink gins, I remember that one is supposed to salute the flag. My slight elbow nudge and a whisper 'Salute,' reminds the general of the required ceremonial.

May 1948

The PRC is almost at its end and so is my army career. My posting in the HQ may last no more than a month or two, so I opt for demob before the summer in order to start my new life in Leven as a photographer. There are no parties or celebrations, just warm handshakes from the superiors and warmer ones from friends. Issued are the demob suit and shoes, a travel warrant and a slip of paper saying that:

No. POLISH / 1599 Captain Szczygieł W. is proceeding from Whitburn to his home address at 17 Scoonie Rd. Leven on his demob.

Separated by the River Rhine

Translation of an article by Wiesław Szczygieł published in *Polska Walcząca* (*Fighting Poland*) 29th September 1945

Arnhem ablaze. At its feet the river Rhine reflects the raging fires. The river separates us from our British comrades at arms. By now they have been fighting for several days, and are impatiently waiting for our help to capture the river crossing so important for the further progress of the land forces.

The British units did not manage to hold the ferry on the river which we were to use immediately after our landing. Their further efforts to organise a crossing for us were also unsuccessful. Now it is our turn to organise our own crossing. It is our sappers' turn. It is well known that sappers are experts at river crossing but it is not so simple for paratroop sappers. In spite of our training, nobody foresaw that we might have to force a river in Holland and nobody thought of equipping us with pontoons or assault boats. Now we miss not having them. The only rubber dinghies which we managed to get hold of were too small. Other larger ones were useful for the rescue of ditching airmen in the North Sea but pretty useless for crossing the fast flowing Rhine.

The enemy, well established on both sides on the narrow perimeter held by the British paras, is not asleep and keeps sending in our direction multicoloured fireworks in various sizes of metal packages. From behind the dyke parallel to the river's edge appear the improvised rafts and dinghies carried by the paras. It is not easy to carry over an uneven terrain the clumsy rafts creaking with every step. The first raft reaches the water's edge. The shore here is flat, just covered by the water; underneath is a muddy bottom. The raft sticks in the mud and is useless.

'Abandon rafts! Use only dinghies,' comes an order from the officer in charge of the crossing.

It is easier to launch and load the dinghies. The paratroopers, encouraged by the sappers, wade knee-deep so that the dinghies do not settle on the muddy bottom. 'Set off' comes a whispered command. The yellow 'tubs' disappear into a momentary darkness. One only hears the gentle noise of spades used as oars.

Shimmering with bluish brightness, an illuminating flare rises above the river, and the officer commanding the crossing sees the yellow dinghies floating down river instead of across. Obviously, the round shape of the boat and the improvised paddles cannot conquer the strong current. Another few hundred metres and they will land in German hands.

You cannot hide on the water surface from an illuminating flare hanging motionless on a small parachute, so over the surface of the water run multi-coloured strings of tracers from machineguns. After a while, everything dies in darkness just to burst in flashes of mortar fire. Will they reach the British parameter? That is the question on everybody's mind. Occasionally a silence reigns but is soon broken by a longer or shorter burst of machinegun. You don't see where it is coming from but you hear it as if it was just within an arm's reach. You can even hear an occasional rattle of the gun's breach in the break between the series. A sensitive ear recognizes all sounds at night, especially over the water.

'Did you hear? It has jammed again … '

'Attention! Ready for another series … ' and a new string of the deadly beads crosses the river.

A new group of soldiers is ready for loading and the moments of anxiety seem to last forever. From behind us, at last, our artillery opens up. You can hear the friendly rounds overhead giving us hope that they will silence the enemy. Unfortunately, there are good and bad results to this. Our artillery sets fire to buildings on the enemy's shore and the fires illuminate the river. But the crossing continues.

In the flickering redness of the fires, some silhouettes appear on our shore. The dinghies come back for loading but one is damaged by shrapnel and is sinking. Only two remain. The enemy fire intensifies, helped by the visibility created by the blazes. The enemy can see most of our movements and pours all the fire available. Machineguns fire continuously, mortar bombs whistle and burst among us, but even more terrifying are the shrapnel rounds of artillery. The whole crossing area is under fire, from loading points, through to starting areas, to waiting lines.

'Stretcher-bearer! Stretcher-bearer!' calls resound. The wounded are carried to relative safety behind the dykes.

The sappers, wet from water and perspiration, load the remaining two dinghies and set off into the unknown. How far will the current carry them? How deadly will the enemy fire be? This seems to last for hours, but at last a runner appears with an order from the HQ: 'Stop crossing at dawn.' The sky begins to brighten, the glare of fires fades with the approaching dawn. We can carry no more. Tomorrow night we will start afresh: the same hell or worse as the enemy will know exactly our narrow loading area and the Spandaus and mortars will have fixed their firing lines.

The Bay of Biscay

Squadron Leader Lesław Międzybrodzki AFC RAF

Extract from *Destiny Can Wait. The Polish Air Force in the Second World War*

It was on 5th May 1944 that the duty officer of No 304 Squadron woke the OC in the night and reported: 'N for Nun' is attacking two U-boats, Flt. Lt Międzybrodzki, sir.'

The German fighters were out in force over the Bay of Biscay that night. Hence the crew of 'N for Nun' flew as low as possible just over the waves. The patrol had already lasted six hours, and the crew could hardly keep their eyes open.

The operator contacted a U-boat at 03.15 hours. The crew livened up in a flash, and the Wellington made straight for the enemy. From behind the clouds the moon appeared, and its silvery light threw a long, brilliant reflection on the water, so bright as to dazzle the eyes. Foam dashing against a darkish object could be seen and just behind this, another dark object. A double sighting!

The wireless ticked out its message to base as the ponderous Leigh Light was slowly lowered into position. The aircraft shook violently as the number of revolutions suddenly increased and the pilot began to run up. The U-boats were moving quickly, low in the water and ready to crash dive at a moment's notice.

The bomb doors opened with a clatter when something flashed inside the fuselage. Flames appeared amidst dense, black, choking smoke. An immediate decision had to be made: to attack or to save the aircraft.

'I'm attacking', said the pilot quietly, 'put out the fire, if you can. Light on!'

The sharp, violet-tinged cone of the searchlight slid across the waves and rested on a U-boat. A tremendous cannonade of flak – cannon, machine guns and pom-poms – was immediately directed against 'N for Nun'. Sharp acrid smoke biting away at tired eyes and making breathing difficult; the heavy flack barrage from the U-boat; a fire on board the aircraft and the calm, unhurried voice of the pilot: 'Co-pilot, give them a burst – I'm attacking.'

As the front machine gun opened fire, the other U-boat joined in the flack barrage. There was no time for evasive action – to interrupt the attack when so close to the U-boat was unthinkable. The pilot peered through the open window of his cockpit, his blood-shot eyes streaming with tears. His fingers pressed the depth-charge release button.

A violent bump, a flash, explosions and darkness. 'N for Nun' was thrown to starboard so that the tip of the wing on that side grazed the water. Black waves leapt viciously at the aircraft as the pilot sharply pulled back on the control column and pushed over the rudder bar as far as possible. 'N for Nun' vibrated above the zero mark as the Wellington turned to port out of the barrage and began to circle.

The wireless operator reported briefly: 'the radio short-circuited, but the fire's out. Everything OK now.' And then the rear gunner's voice: 'Charges straddled the Jerry all right.'

'N for Nun' kept turning, struggled to climb, seemed to hang suspended on its maimed wings, but inch by inch, yard by yard, height was gained.

A red rocket shot up high in the air from the spot where the attack had been made. By its light the crew saw the U-boat disappear under the waves. Its lines looked strangely distorted and bent. One of the charges must have made a direct hit. The other U-boat cruised around for ten minutes or so and then submerged. There were no survivors to pick up, and it returned to port alone.

'N for Nun' limped to base, and touched down in early morning in heavy rain and in the teeth of a near gale. The Wellington was a pitiful sight. Filthy with the soot of explosions and fire, bespattered with oil, it had lost all its cool virgin whiteness. The rear turret was full of holes and the elevator trimming tabs were torn. The starboard wing had been badly damaged by a cannon shell, and the ground crews wondered why the whole wing had not fallen off on the way. In addition, between the engine nacelle and the fuselage there was a hole big enough for a man to pass through.'

Destiny Can Wait. The History of the Polish Air Force Association in Great Britain, published *by* William Heinemann. Reprinted by permission of The Random House Group Ltd.

Squadron Leader Lesław Międzybrodzki AFC RAF

End Piece

Professor Emeritus Peter H Jones FRSE

The invariable challenge to historians of the past is this: they were not there. But those who have spoken today, together with their colleagues whose reminiscences we have read, were there. It is a privilege beyond value to be in the presence of men and women without whom none of us would be here. For those of us who can only wonder at the courage and integrity of our veterans, the horrors and loss they endured can only be imagined.

First, the horror: and the unspeakable absurdity of the concentration camps. And then the inconsequentiality and impromptu character of the war: a short sight seeing trip to Venice, or an excursion into the bowels of Versailles. And, most humbling of all, the human spirit, and its capacity to surmount even Scottish wartime food, and the wet.

In the West, the traditions of oral history and story telling are all but lost. The increasing domination of the text since the eighteenth century, and the high premium properly placed on reading skills, have separated us both from our past and from three quarters of the world's present population. Probably no-one amongst us retains the capacity of our ancestors to recall, retain and re-tell at length what we hear; alongside our inability to recall accurately any long speech goes our inability to listen for any length of time. All teachers know, and are repeatedly taught, that attention spans at all ages seem nowadays to be remarkably short. But it was not always so, and it is not so in many parts of the developing world. The issue is important for a very simple reason. Conversation is itself a sacred practice in which the duty to listen precedes the right to speak. Our ability to listen determines our ability to remember; and our memories constitute the very anchor of our lives, and of society in general. On the basis of our memories alone, we can understand our debts and our heritage; and only by grasping our debts can we sustain the values of our ancestors, and fulfil our duties both to them and to our successors.

By sharing their memories, and by inviting us to enter the treasury of their private worlds, our veterans have paid us a moving compliment; for civic society can be animated, and can evolve in response to change, only if its memories are cherished and its values re-affirmed. Their compliment, however, is as nothing beside our debt.

PHJ

The units of the 1st Polish Independent Parachute Brigade on parade

The units of the 1st Polish Independent Parachute Brigade on parade
(© Fife Council Museums East)

The Colours of the 1st Polish Parachute Brigade on parade (© Fife Council Museums East)

The Scots at War Trust Seminar

Polish Forces in Scotland

Headquarters 2nd Division Craigiehall, Edinburgh
Thursday 2nd November 2000

In the presence of
HRH The Prince Philip, Duke of Edinburgh KG KT
Patron of The Scots at War Trust

Participants

HRH The Prince Philip, Duke of Edinburgh

Captain T Apfel-Czaszka, Veteran of the Polish Armoured Division

Mr Zbigniew Budzyński, Veteran of the Polish 5th Infantry Division

Mr Allan Carswell, Curator, National War Museum of Scotland

Mr Douglas A Connell WS, Legal Adviser to The Scots at War Trust

Brigadier Frank Coutts KOSB, Veteran of the 52nd Lowland Division

Mr Tam Dalyell MP, Member of Parliament for West Lothian

Mr Aleksander Dietkow, Consul General of the Republic of Poland

Dr Kazimierz Piotr Durkacz, Veteran of the Polish Army and Graduate of the Polish School of Medicine at The University of Edinburgh

Miss Nicola Flynn, Pupil of Inveralmond Community High School

Major General R D S Gordon, GOC 2nd Division

General Sir Michael Gow, Chairman of The Scots at War Trust

Lt Colonel George Harvey, Veteran of the Polish Parachute Brigade

Miss Paula Head-Fourman, Pupil, Fettes College

Dr Diana M Henderson, Trustee and Honorary Research Director of the Scots at War Trust

Mr Douglas Johnson, The Royal British Legion, Scotland

Squadron Leader Lynda Johnson RAF, Equerry in Waiting

Professor Emeritus Peter H Jones, Trustee and Honorary Treasurer of the Scots at War Trust

Mr Stefan Kay, son of a Polish Veteran

Mrs Elizabeth Kendzia, Veteran Red Cross VAD Ambulance Driver for the Polish Forces in Fife

HE Dr Stanisław Komorowski, Ambassador of the Republic of Poland

Lt Colonel J J Korabiowski, Veteran of the 4th Polish Infantry Division

Mr J A Leszczuk, Teacher of History, Inveralmond Community High School, Livingstone, and son of a Polish Veteran

Miss Morna Liddle, Pupil, Inveralmond Community High School

Admiral Sir Michael Livesay, Chairman of The Royal British Legion, Scotland, and Trustee of the Scots at War Trust

Squadron Leader Międzybrodzki, Veteran of 304 (Polish) Squadron, Royal Air Force

Colonel Alan R Miller, Deputy Chief of Staff, 2nd Division

Mr Lech S Muszyński, Veteran of the 7th Polish Division

Mr Raymond Muszyński, son of a Polish Veteran

Mr Robert Ostrycharz, Polish Forces Historian and Vice Chairman of the General Sikorski Memorial House, Glasgow

Mr Mark Peel, Teacher of History, Fettes College

Mr Sam Phipps, Journalist
Mr Trevor Royle, Writer, Historian and Journalist
Lt Colonel Ian Shepherd, Secretary, Scottish National War Memorial
Major General Sir John Swinton, Chairman of Trustees of Scottish National War Memorial and Trustee of the Scots at War Trust
Mr Oliver Thring, Pupil, Fettes College
Miss Yvonne Wilson, Pupil, Inveralmond High School
Colonel M H White, MS to GOC 2nd Division
Major Hugh Young, Protocol Officer 2nd Division
Mr Michael Zawada, Veteran of the Polish Navy

The event was sponsored by The Kintore Charitable Trust

The Scots at War Trust
Flat No 5
2 Barnton Avenue West
Edinburgh EH4 6EB
www-saw.arts.ed.ac.uk
dianahenderson@ukonline.co.uk

Books from Cualann Press

Open Road to Faraway
Escapes from Nazi POW Camps 1941-1945
Andrew S Winton D A (Edin)
Foreword: Allan Carswell, Curator of the National War Museum of Scotland
ISBN: 0 9535036 5 8   £9.99

Stand By Your Beds!
A Wry Look at National Service
David Findlay Clark OBE, MA, Ph.D., C.Psychol., F.B.Ps.S.
Preface: Trevor Royle
ISBN: 0 9535036 6 6   £13.99

Beyond the Bamboo Screen
Scottish Prisoners of War under the Japanese
Extracts from Newsletters of the Scottish Far East Prisoner of War Association
and Other Sources
Tom McGowran OBE   Illustrations by G S Gimson QC
ISBN 0 9535036 1 5   Price £9.99

On Flows the Tay
Perth and the First World War
Dr Bill Harding Ph.D., FEIS
ISBN 0 9535036 2 3   Price £12.99

Under the Shadow
Letters of Love and War
The Poignant Testimony and Story of Hugh Wallace Mann and Jessie Reid
Narrative: Bríd Hetherington
ISBN 0 9535036 0 7   Price £12.99

Of Fish and Men
Tales of a Scottish Fisher
David C Watson
Foreword: Derek Mills
ISBN 09535036 3 1   Price £10.99